2ND EDITION

Rules in School

Teaching Discipline in the
Responsive Classroom®

KATHRYN BRADY   MARY BETH FORTON   DEBORAH PORTER

All net proceeds from the sale of this book support the work of Northeast Foundation for Children, Inc. (NEFC). NEFC, a not-for-profit educational organization, is the developer of the *Responsive Classroom*® approach to teaching, which fosters safe, challenging, and joyful elementary classrooms and schools.

The stories in this book are all based on real events in the classroom. However, in order to respect the privacy of students, names and many identifying characteristics of students and situations have been changed.

ISBN: 978-1-892989-42-0

Library of Congress control number: 2010932147

Cover photographs: © Alice Proujansky, Jeff Woodward, and Peter Wrenn. All rights reserved.

Interior photographs: © Marlynn K. Clayton, Alice Proujansky, Elizabeth Willis, Jeff Woodward, and Peter Wrenn. All rights reserved.

Cover and book design: Helen Merena

We would like to thank the teachers and students who so graciously welcomed Northeast Foundation for Children to take pictures in their classrooms.

Northeast Foundation for Children, Inc.
85 Avenue A, Suite 204
P. O. Box 718
Turners Falls, MA 01376-0718

800-360-6332
www.responsiveclassroom.org

16 15 14 13 12   7 6 5 4 3 2

Printed on recycled paper

Note from the Editor about the Second Edition

The *Responsive Classroom®* approach is dynamic. Although our core foundational beliefs have remained steady, specifics of our practice have developed and evolved to better meet the needs of teachers and students.

Rules in School was first published in 2002. Since that time we've refined our thinking about teaching discipline and those changes are reflected in this second edition. Also, *Rules in School* is now focused specifically on classroom discipline strategies and no longer has a chapter on discipline outside the classroom. We have greatly developed our thinking about schoolwide discipline and in 2011 will be publishing a book on the topic, co-authored by Chip Wood and Babs Freeman-Loftis.

Additional changes include:

- We have placed greater emphasis on the need for teaching and reinforcing the positive behaviors that are essential to effective teaching and learning.

- We have refined our articulation of how to use role-playing to help prepare students for complex social situations.

- We have included updated resources.

Working on the second edition of *Rules in School* has been an exciting process because it has kept me in touch with the vital interaction between a book and its audience. I hope you enjoy this book and find it a useful guide to creating a safe and peaceful classroom.

Lynn Bechtel
Senior Editor, Northeast Foundation for Children
August 2010

19.21.14

This book is dedicated to teachers everywhere
for believing deeply in the goodness of children,
even when the going gets tough.

TABLE OF CONTENTS

Overview of the *Responsive Classroom*® Approach to Discipline

"Rules are bad," announced my four-year-old son with an indignant "Humph!" when I told him I was working on a book on rules in school. "You want to do something and the teacher just comes along and says you can't!"

This is clearly a four-year-old point of view—I want what I want and I want it now and anything that gets in my way is bad. But it's a point of view shared by many students in elementary schools, where rules are often seen as adversarial, as decrees handed down from the authorities above to keep you from doing what you want.

The teacher announces the rules on the first day of school with little or no discussion of their meaning. The message is clear: Follow these rules or else. While this approach to rule setting can be effective in establishing a sense of order in a classroom (which we very much need), it does little to help children develop self-discipline, ethical thinking, or an understanding of how to be contributing members of a democratic community. At its worst, it invites tension, blind obedience, or a constant battle of wills between adults and children in school.

1

This book offers a different approach to classroom discipline. It's an approach that has helped teachers in a wide range of elementary school settings establish calm and safe classrooms while helping children develop self-discipline and a sense of responsibility. It reflects the beliefs that discipline is a subject that can be "taught," just as we teach reading and writing and math, and that children learn best when they're actively engaged and invested in constructing their own understandings.

This is not a new approach to discipline. It's been used since 1981 by many teachers using the *Responsive Classroom* approach to teaching (see the page titled "About the *Responsive Classroom*® Approach" at the end of this book).

The primary goals of this approach are to:

- Establish a calm, orderly, and safe environment for learning

- Help children develop self-control and self-discipline

- Teach children to be responsible, contributing members of a democratic community

- Promote respectful, kind, and healthy teacher–student and student–student interactions

In classrooms using this approach to discipline, rules are connected to students' and teachers' goals for social and academic learning. Often, the rules are created collaboratively with students and teachers during the early weeks of school. While there will always be times when students don't like following the rules or choose not to follow them, students in these schools generally view rules in a positive light. They understand that the rules are there to keep them safe and help them achieve their goals in school.

As one third grader so clearly put it, "Rules in school are good because they help keep kids safe and in control so they can learn. But I'm glad at my school there isn't too many rules. Just a few good ones."

In the chapters that follow you'll learn practical strategies for establishing clear behavior expectations and teaching students how to achieve these expectations. You will also learn tools and techniques for how to respond when children misbehave.

The first three chapters provide an overview of the tools and techniques, grades K–8. The following three chapters show these tools and techniques being used at specific grade levels: K–2, 3–5, and 6–8. Each of these chapters is written by a teacher at that grade level: Deborah Porter for grades K–2 and Kathryn Brady for grades 3–5 and 6–8.

Three Common Approaches to Discipline

Following is an overview of three approaches to discipline often used in classrooms and schools and how they differ from the approach described in this book.

An autocratic approach: "Because I said so!"

Some of us are familiar with an autocratic approach to discipline from our own years in school, where we encountered a long list of rules, often stated in the negative and with a high premium on being quiet and still. These rules were meant to keep us in line. They appeared magically on the first day of school and few dared to question them. It wasn't important that students understood the rules. It was just important to follow them.

Implicit was the notion that without the rules, our natural impulses would take hold and at any moment chaos would erupt: Just imagine thirty children racing around the classroom, screaming at the top of their lungs, gum dropping from their mouths, pushing and fighting with one another.

This approach to discipline is still at work in classrooms today. One of the key assumptions behind this approach is that children are by nature unruly and impulsive—largely incapable of self-regulation—and it's the teacher's responsibility to make them behave. Left to their own devices, children will most likely do the wrong thing.

Many children opt to comply in an autocratic system, but largely out of fear of what will happen to them if they don't. Others become masterful at putting on a good show for the teacher while completely disregarding the rules when no one's looking. Still others become extremely resistant and defiant or, in the other extreme, so completely dependent on adults to guide their behavior that they find it impossible to make ethical decisions on their own.

This approach can achieve an orderly classroom, but at what cost? An approach to discipline that's based on fear and punishment externally controls children but does little to teach them self-control. It achieves compliance but it also yields anxiety, resentment, and anger. While the classroom might appear calm and productive on the outside, students often feel humiliated, afraid, and resentful on the inside, hardly optimal conditions for learning.

A permissive approach: "Can you please cooperate now, please?"

On the other end of the spectrum is a permissive approach to rules and discipline where there are no clear limits for behavior. Here rules are negotiable and easily bendable. They may be clearly stated and posted in a prominent place in the room, but everyone knows they won't be enforced consistently.

Teachers using this approach may believe that the most important thing is for children to like them. They may put a high premium on being nice and may worry about stifling or alienating their students by being too hard on them. Or they might believe that the best way to influence children's behavior is to ignore undesirable actions while reinforcing desirable ones with generous doses of praise. Or perhaps they've experienced the negative effects of an autocratic approach and don't want to inflict it on others.

Whatever the underlying intention, a permissive approach leads to many problems. Among them, small disturbances routinely escalate into bigger ones, conflicts are unresolved, and rudeness, teasing, and taunting go unchecked, leaving many children feeling physically and psychologically unsafe. If somehow students are behaving in such a classroom, they're often doing so only to please the teacher and win the teacher's approval.

Students in these classrooms can feel just as fearful, tense, and dependent as those in classrooms using an autocratic approach, says Deborah Porter, longtime primary grade teacher. "Instead of being confined by an overly controlling teacher, these students are crippled by the lack of clear boundaries and structure," she says. "We might think that having no limits and no adult guidance makes children feel free, but it actually makes them feel tense and out of control. They're always trying to figure out what's acceptable and what isn't."

Teachers hold so little authority in these classrooms that when they do need to gain control of the classroom, they often resort to pleading, cajoling, or bribing to try to convince students to cooperate. One risk is that these teachers will grow so thoroughly discouraged by students' behavior and the lack of cooperation that they decide to quit teaching altogether.

A flip-flop approach: "I said, 'No.' Well, maybe one more chance. Now, that's it. I mean 'No.'"

There are teachers, many of them in their early years of teaching and without any support around classroom management, who bounce back and forth between the autocratic and permissive extremes. This is perhaps the worst kind of discipline, with the complete lack of predictability and consistency leading to confusion, frustration, and anxiety for students and teachers alike.

I'll never forget my own early years in a classroom, teaching language arts six periods a day to twenty-five to thirty eighth graders. The summer before starting, I spent many hours preparing exciting lessons on literature, creative writing, and journalism. I reflected on my own years in junior high school and reminded myself of all the things I didn't want to be as a teacher. I would not lecture, yell, dominate, or humiliate. I would not put the desks in rows or insist on quiet and solitary work. I would not fill the days with mundane busywork and worksheets.

I didn't spend much time thinking about how I would approach discipline. I figured that by now the students would know what was expected of them. Besides, they'd be so excited by what they were learning there wouldn't be much need to talk about anything as routine and mundane as rules.

I envisioned a vibrant classroom, full of lively debates, plays, poetry readings, and engaging conversations about literature. Students would be self-motivated and industrious. The room would be orderly and calm yet buzzing with the excitement of learning. Students and teachers would treat each other with kindness and respect.

These were great intentions but I didn't have a chance of pulling them off. With little supervision and no roadmaps for creating the social climate I wanted, I bounced back and forth between being permissive and being strict, being nice and being mean, pleading and punishing. I knew full well that what I was doing was ineffective, but I didn't have the strategies or guidance I needed to change it.

The lack of clarity made the classroom tense. Students became increasingly impulsive and testy, always searching for limits that didn't exist or that changed daily. The lively conversations and debates I envisioned became free-for-alls with students interrupting and talking over one another, putting each other down, and laughing at each other's mistakes.

With so few tools to draw on, I watched in horror as I saw myself becoming the teacher I never wanted to be—yelling, lecturing, humiliating, pushing desks back into neat rows, and preparing mounds of busywork just to keep things under control. While I knew there must be a better way, I had so little experience or guidance in how to create a calm, safe, and orderly climate without resorting to punishment or humiliation that I felt demoralized and ready to give up.

My story is hardly unique. Although new teachers may have learned about classroom management in teacher education coursework, actually managing twenty-five or more students in a small space for seven hours a day can be challenging, especially if teachers lack mentoring or administrative support.

But it's not only new teachers who face this challenge. Experienced teachers, too, can feel overwhelmed by the demands placed on them as more and more students come to school with poorly developed social skills, a lack of impulse control, and few tools to handle their anger and frustration.

Discipline in our nation's classrooms and schools is clearly a pressing concern and an important factor in students' success. How teachers approach discipline can make all the difference between whether children feel safe or threatened in our schools, motivated or discouraged, successful or defeated. It can determine whether a classroom will be orderly or chaotic and whether children will learn or flounder. Ultimately it impacts whether teachers feel fulfilled or frustrated, whether they like their work, and whether they stay in the teaching profession.

Discipline in the *Responsive Classroom* Approach

The approach to discipline described in this book is neither autocratic nor permissive. Often referred to as an efficacious, positive, or judicious approach, it aims to help children develop self-control, begin to understand what socially responsible behavior is, and come to value such behavior.

This approach to discipline does not rely on punishment or rewards to "get students to behave." Neither does it ignore behavior that is detrimental to the child or to the group. Rather, this approach offers clear expectations for behavior and actively teaches children how to live up to those expectations.

Teachers using this approach help children become aware of how their actions can bring positive and negative consequences to themselves and

others. When children misbehave, teachers use respectful strategies to stop the misbehavior and restore positive behavior as quickly as possible so that children can continue to learn and the teacher can continue to teach.

Teachers strive to be firm, kind, and consistent. Their aim is to create calm, safe, and orderly classrooms while preserving the dignity of each child. This requires a constant balancing of the needs of the group with the needs of the individual, the need for order with the need for movement and activity, the need for teachers to be in control of the classroom with the need for students to be in control of their own lives and learning. It requires taking the time to teach children how to be contributing members of a caring learning community.

Just as teachers don't expect children to come to school knowing how to read or write, teachers using this approach don't make assumptions about the social skills children bring to school. Some children will come to school with highly developed social skills and many years of experience being part of a large group. Others will need to start from the beginning.

School provides an ideal setting for social learning. There are endless opportunities at school for children to learn to control their impulses and to think about the needs and feelings of others. Whether they're learning to wait their turn to talk, ask politely for a marker, welcome a newcomer into a group, or disagree with someone's ideas without attacking them personally, school is rich with opportunities for children to learn to think and act in socially responsible ways.

The time teachers spend on classroom discipline is an investment that will be richly repaid. As long-time teacher Ruth Sidney Charney writes in *Teaching Children to Care*, "I've grown to appreciate the task of helping children take better care of themselves, of each other, and of their classrooms. It's not a waste. It's probably the most enduring thing I teach." (Charney, 2002, p. 18)

WORK CITED

Charney, Ruth Sidney. (2002). *Teaching Children to Care: Classroom Management for Ethical and Academic Growth, K–8*. Greenfield, MA: Northeast Foundation for Children, Inc.

Creating Rules with Students

Purposes and Reflections

Walk into any classroom using the *Responsive Classroom* approach to discipline and one of the things you'll notice is a chart of three to five rules such as "Respect each other"; "Take care of yourself"; "Take care with classroom property." Rather than listing all the possible dos and don'ts, these rules remind students in a global way of what they should do. Connected to student and teacher goals and often created with the students, these rules set limits and boundaries but do so in a way that fosters group ownership.

Why is it important to keep the rules positive, broad, and few in number? I remember a visit I once made to a retreat center that had long lists of rules posted everywhere. Don't leave the door open, don't leave the water running, don't make any long distance calls, don't, don't, don't. At first I felt nervous about these rules. What if I don't remember? Then I felt annoyed. How can they expect me to remember all of these? I even felt a bit rebellious. I'll leave the water running if I feel like it. How would they know anyway? Finally, there were so many rules posted in so many places that I just stopped paying attention.

Children, too, become overwhelmed or resentful when they are handed long lists of dos and don'ts. Many will decide they have license to do anything that isn't specifically prohibited: Think of the all-too-familiar "But teacher, it doesn't say I can't. . . ."

11

By contrast, rules that are few in number, global in scope, and clearly connected to learning goals are likely to be respected. Challenging and guiding students to make good decisions, these rules become the cornerstone of classroom life.

Goals of classroom rules

The goals of creating rules in the *Responsive Classroom* approach to discipline are as follows:

- Establish guidelines and expectations for positive behavior

- Create a sense of order and safety—both physical and psychological— in the classroom

- Teach children the purpose of rules by connecting the rules to learning goals

Steps in creating rules

Rule creation takes place in the early weeks of school and does require an investment of time. However, teachers find over and over that the payoffs in increased student responsibility and decreased problem behaviors are well worth the effort.

The process typically involves the following steps:

1. ***Articulating learning goals.*** The teacher asks students to share their learning goals for the school year, often beginning the conversation by sharing her own goals. Families are also invited to share their goals for their child.

2. ***Generating rules.*** The teacher and children collaborate to generate rules that will allow everyone to achieve their learning goals for the year.

3. ***Framing the rules in the positive.*** The teacher works with students to turn the rules into positive statements.

4. *Condensing the list down to a few global rules.* The teacher and students work together to consolidate their long list of specific rules so they end up with three to five global classroom rules.

Having faith in children's abilities to make sense of the rules

To be successful in creating rules with students, teachers must have faith that children can make sense of the rules and want to follow them. In spite of all the alarming news reports about violence and irreverence in schools, it's important to keep in mind that most children, most of the time, want to and do follow the rules, especially rules they view as reasonable and fair.

Not only are children amenable to rules, they crave them. Rules give children a sense of security in an often confusing and unpredictable world. Even in the earliest grades, children can understand that rules are there to help them learn and grow. While they may sometimes resent following rules, especially in moments of anger or frustration, they can understand that rules help make their classroom a good place to be—a place that is safe, kind, and orderly.

William Damon, a developmental psychologist and author of *The Moral Child*, reminds us that "all children are born with a running start to moral development." But, he asserts, it's the social influences in a child's life that shape that moral development. (Damon, 1999) And school is one of the most important of these social influences. As teachers, it's our job to help nurture children's moral development. Taking the time to create rules with students and expecting students to live by them is one way of doing that.

When rules make sense: A family story

When I was ten years old, something happened that helped me really understand the purpose of rules.

One day, a day not unlike most in a house filled with five energetic school-age children, my father became fed up with the way we all left trails of books, coats, shoes, papers, food, and toys in our wake. While the rules of the house were clear on this matter, more often than not we chose to ignore them, and no amount of nagging, cajoling, or reprimanding seemed to help. Eventually we would get around to picking things up or they would magically disappear overnight with a little help from our parents. But this day my father decided that a new approach was needed. What was missing, he realized, was an appreciation for the rule itself.

He called us down to the living room and soberly announced that as of the next morning there would be no more rules about leaving books, toys, coats, food, etc., around the house. From now on, we could leave things anywhere we wanted and no one was going to pick them up.

It was an interesting week. No more nagging when we dropped our books and coats on the floor after coming home from school, no more reminders to clean up one game or art project before taking out another. We giggled as we deliberately abandoned plates of half-eaten snacks on the coffee table and dramatically dropped shoes and sports equipment in the middle of the living room floor. Freedom at last!

After several days the house became a total mess, every room and hallway littered with our things and our trash. The sense of order that we were so accustomed to was suddenly gone and we began to grow uneasy. The novelty had worn off and we began to wonder when the game would stop.

Oddly our parents seemed not to notice. They calmly stepped over our debris, gently nudged a bag or toy to make their way up the stairs, silently moved a plate of crusty food to make room for their mug. Finally, after six days of this, we children couldn't stand it anymore. The chaos was beginning to interfere with our lives, not only making it hard to find things when we needed them but making it hard to feel any sense of order or stability. We begged our parents to end their silence and put the rules back in place.

What followed was the first meaningful discussion I had ever had about rules. What should the rule be? Why do we need this rule? How should it be enforced?

For the first time in my life it dawned on me that rules were there to help us, not to control or stifle or irritate us. What a revelation this was!

And what a difference it made in my willingness to follow rules, at least the ones that made sense to me.

Getting Started

It's the first day of school and students walk into their classrooms full of anxiety, uncertainty, and a million questions: What will my new teacher be like? Will she be nice? Will she be in control of the class? What do we do if we need to go the bathroom? Will the other kids be friendly? Do I have to stay at my desk? Will there be a lot of homework? What are the rules here?

Like master detectives, the children search the classroom, the walls, the books, the teacher's tone of voice, the other students' movements, for clues to answer these and other questions. What they want to know is what will reign in this place. Order or chaos? Kindness or cruelty? Calmness or confusion? Respect for materials or reckless abandonment?

By the end of the first few days, many students will have formed conclusions about what kind of year this will be. They'll know whether the teacher feels confident or shaky. They'll know whether the classroom feels friendly or mean. And they'll have a pretty good sense of whether they will be held to high academic and social standards.

We all need this kind of information in new situations. Whether we walk into a new job, a new neighborhood, or a new country, as social beings we need to know the customs and codes of conduct of our new environment. But children especially crave this kind of information, and they need it during the first few days of school.

The first priority: Establish a sense of calm and order

Before ever beginning a discussion of classroom rules, it's essential to create a sense of order, predictability, and trust in the classroom. From day one, teachers need to convey the message that in this classroom, respect, kindness, and learning will prevail. Students need to know in no uncertain terms that the teacher is in control and that the standards for behavior are high. This knowledge gives students a sense of physical and emotional security. It also frees them to participate in rule creation and other class-room activities in a meaningful way.

This point cannot be emphasized enough. Teachers who breeze over establishing order and jump too quickly to creating rules with students often find that the process backfires. When students don't feel safe, they won't invest in rule creation. The conversations become confusing, superficial, even farcical, with students challenging the process every step of the way. "Why are we making the rules? Isn't that your job?" they demand. "We don't care about the stupid rules. Let's make a rule that says we'll have no rules."

So, how do teachers establish order and safety? They explicitly introduce behavior expectations and routines—all the basics from how to respond to a signal for quiet and how to line up, to what's expected at cleanup, to what to do if you finish your work early. The way in which they approach this and the amount of time needed vary according to children's developmental level and experience with routines from other grades—but children of all ages will benefit from time spent on establishing order from day one.

(For a more detailed discussion of how to create order, security, and community during the early weeks of school, please see *The First Six Weeks of School* by Paula Denton and Roxann Kriete.)

Model routine behaviors

Children are able, even eager, to rise to high standards of behavior, but they need to know exactly what the standards are. If we expect students to walk instead of run when moving around the room, put away materials after using them, keep their hands to themselves in the meeting area, share materials, raise their hand to speak, help to put away the sports equipment, and show attention and interest when a classmate is talking, then we have to be clear and direct about these expectations.

Interactive modeling is a good technique for teaching these expectations during the first few days of school. Simple and direct, it's used to teach the non-negotiable behaviors and routines that help keep the classroom running smoothly and safely. Here are some typical routines taught in the early days of school:

- Responding to a signal for quiet (see page 21)
- Carrying chairs in the classroom
- Sharpening a pencil
- Lining up
- Using the drinking fountain
- Walking down the hall
- Going through the cafeteria line
- Hanging up coats
- Wiping off tables
- Asking to use or borrow materials
- Carrying scissors
- Walking through the classroom
- Putting things away in a cubby or storage area
- Listening to a speaker

Interactive modeling can be used effectively with children in all elementary grades. The technique may seem at first most suitable for younger children, for whom many everyday routines are still new. But with some adjustments in language and pacing, it can be invaluable for students in upper grades as well.

Interactive modeling conveys the message that in this classroom, everyone is expected to carry out all everyday activities in a safe and responsible way. And it explicitly teaches children the skills they need to do so. Through interactive modeling, children learn what positive behavior looks like, sounds like, and feels like.

Steps in interactive modeling

The technique typically includes the following six steps:

1. **Describe the positive behavior to be modeled.** When appropriate, connect the behavior to an established expectation.

2. **Demonstrate the behavior.** Sometimes, if students are familiar with the positive behavior, teachers might ask for suggestions of what to do.

3. **Ask students what they noticed about the demonstrated behavior.** Elicit observations about specific actions, expressions, and tone of voice.

4. **Ask student volunteers to demonstrate the same behavior.** Be sure to alert students to once again pay attention to specific aspects of how the modelers do the behavior.

5. **Ask students what they noticed.** Again elicit observations about specific actions, expressions, and tone of voice.

6. **Students practice; teacher observes and coaches, using reinforcing language.** The teacher observes and guides children in their practice, using reinforcing language to support their positive efforts. The teacher also lets the students know that practice and coaching will be ongoing as students interact with each other in the coming days and weeks.

Interactive modeling in action

In the following pages, you'll see examples of interactive modeling used during the early days of school at two grade levels, second grade and fifth grade.

A SECOND GRADE CLASS
LEARNS HOW TO LISTEN ATTENTIVELY

1. ***The teacher describes a positive behavior to be modeled.*** "Many times during our school day we'll be listening to each other share news and ideas and it's important that we listen attentively and respectfully."

2. ***The teacher demonstrates the behavior.*** The teacher has arranged ahead of time for Kesha to help with today's interactive modeling. Now she says to the class, "Kesha is going to tell me about an upcoming family event. I'll be the listener. Notice what I do." Kesha says that her aunt and new baby cousin are arriving tomorrow for a visit. The teacher listens attentively.

3. ***The teacher asks students what they noticed about the demonstrated behavior.*** "What did I do to show Kesha that I was listening to her?" Students respond, "You looked at her"; "You looked like you were concentrating"; "You didn't move around"; "You nodded your head."

4. ***The teacher asks student volunteers to demonstrate the same behavior.*** "Who else would like to show how to listen in a respectful way?" Randy raises his hand. "OK, this time Randy will be the speaker. He's going to tell about some fun plans he has for the weekend." Another student, Ariela, volunteers to be the listener. The class watches Ariela as Randy shares.

5. ***The teacher asks what students noticed.*** Students share their observations.

6. ***Students practice; the teacher observes and coaches, using reinforcing language.*** "Let's all practice attentive listening now," the teacher says. "I'll share something with you and you can all show how you listen." After the practice, the teacher reinforces the students' listening behavior. "You all sat quietly and many of you were looking at me. I saw a few people nodding as I talked."

The practice doesn't end here, however. The teacher lets students know that she looks forward to seeing them practice respectful listening in the days to come. And when she notices children practicing respectful listening, she continues to use reinforcing language to support the positive behavior.

A FIFTH GRADE CLASS LEARNS HOW TO MOVE SAFELY FROM SMALL-GROUP WORK SPACES TO THE MEETING CIRCLE

1. **The teacher describes a positive behavior to be modeled.** "When we move from the tables to our meeting circle, we need to take care of each other by moving safely."

2. **The teacher demonstrates the behavior.** "Let's say I'm doing my morning work and the teacher says it's time to gather in the circle," the teacher says. She knows that many students experienced this routine in fourth grade and know how to make a safe transition to the meeting circle, so she asks for ideas. "What do I need to do?" The teacher then demonstrates, incorporating the students' suggestions.

3. **The teacher asks students what they noticed about the demonstrated behavior.** "What did you notice about how I moved to the meeting circle?" the teacher asks. Students answer, "You stood up carefully so that you didn't knock the chair over"; "You pushed your chair in"; "You walked to the circle"; "You kept your hands to yourself"; "You didn't push and shove."

4. **The teacher asks for student volunteers to demonstrate the same behavior.** "Now we need one of you to show us how to move safely to the meeting circle." Caren volunteers. Her classmates watch and notice details of what she does.

5. **The teacher asks students what they noticed about the behavior that Caren modeled.** "What did Caren do to keep herself and others safe?" Students answer, "She walked slowly"; "She looked where she was going"; "She didn't fool around."

6. Students practice; the teacher observes and coaches, using reinforcing language. "This week when we move to the meeting circle, let's all pay special attention to how we move safely," the teacher says. "We'll check in on Friday about how we're doing with this."

Here the whole-class practice takes place in the days after the interactive modeling. This can be very effective, as long as the teacher reinforces their ongoing efforts and the class gathers again to reflect on their practice.

Break routines down into manageable steps

Consider breaking down more complex routines into component behaviors with each behavior being introduced and modeled separately. This is especially important in primary grades, when students are often learning routines for the first time. For example, the routine of standing in line could be broken down as follows:

- Paying attention to a signal for quiet

- Moving to the line-up area safely and quietly

- Finding your place in line

- Standing quietly until the teacher gives further instructions

Establish signals for quiet

Students need to know from day one that the teacher has an effective and calm way—something other than yelling—to get their attention. This is not something that needs to be discussed and should never be negotiated. It is an absolutely essential tool for classroom management that should be taught on the first day of school. The teacher might say, "There'll be lots of times when I or someone else in the classroom needs to get your attention. Here are the signals we'll use for that."

Interactive modeling is an effective way to teach signals (see box on page 23 for an example). The signals will vary depending on the age of the students, the location (indoors, outdoors, at the meeting area, etc.), and the style of the teacher. Following, you'll find information about three common signals: a visual signal, an auditory signal for indoor use, and an auditory signal for outdoor use.

A visual signal such as raising a hand

This is used in whole-group meetings or other situations in which everyone can easily see the teacher or whoever needs the group's attention. The person raises a hand. Children who see this may raise their hands as well to help spread the signal. Everyone in the group responds by becoming quiet and turning to the person who wants to speak. This person waits until everyone is paying full attention before beginning.

An auditory signal such as ringing a chime

An auditory signal is most often used when children are spread out in the classroom. When the signal is given, everyone turns to the person who gave the signal and freezes. When finished speaking, the person says something like "You can melt" to signal that students can return to what they were doing. Primary grade teachers often add the step of children folding their arms on their chest when they hear the signal. This helps younger children keep their hands "frozen" and away from tempting materials while listening to the speaker.

A louder auditory signal for outdoor use, such as blowing a whistle or shouting "Circle up!"

Both of these are effective for getting students' attention when outdoors. In either case, the signal means the students should gather around the teacher for further instructions.

How to Respond to a Signal for Quiet

1 *The teacher describes a positive behavior to be modeled.* "There will be times when I need to get your quiet attention. I will raise my hand. When I do that you need to stop whatever you are doing and quietly look at me."

2 *The teacher demonstrates the behavior.* "I've asked Jonas and Margie to help with this demonstration. I'm going to chat with Jonas, like we sometimes do when we first come to the meeting circle, and Margie is going to raise her hand to get our quiet attention. Notice what we do."

3 *The teacher asks students what they noticed about the behavior that was demonstrated.* "What did you notice about how Jonas and I responded when Margie raised her hand?" Students answer, "You stopped talking"; "You turned to look at Margie"; "You didn't fidget around."

4 *The teacher asks for student volunteers to demonstrate the same behavior.* "Now I'd like three volunteers. Two of you will talk and the third person will raise a hand to get your quiet attention." She directs the class to notice what the volunteers do.

5 *The teacher asks students what they noticed about the behavior that the volunteers modeled.* "What did Kylie and Jasmine do when Marcus raised his hand?" Students respond with their observations.

6 *Students practice; the teacher observes and coaches, using reinforcing language.* "Now let's all practice. Turn to your neighbor and talk. When you see me raise my hand, stop talking and quietly turn toward me."

In establishing these signals, it's important to be clear on exactly how they'll be used and why. For example, if the goal is to get everyone's quiet attention, is it okay if students raise their hands when they see the teacher's hand go up, but then continue to talk with a friend? Is it okay to freeze when the bell rings but not look at the person speaking? Is it okay to continue doodling as long as you're looking at the person speaking? Children need clarity about these expectations and the reasons behind them. The more consistent, clear, and firm teachers are, the more useful the signals will be.

Many teachers spend time during the first few days of school practicing these signals. With older students, teachers might issue a challenge: "I'll be using our two signals for quiet a lot over the next few days to help us practice getting quiet and paying attention. Let's see how quickly we all get quiet. I'm going to be timing us every day."

Younger students especially enjoy playing games of freezing and melting to the signal of the bell. During these practice sessions the teacher makes sure to reinforce examples of children following expectations. The more specific and concrete, the better. For example: "People's feet are firmly on the floor when they freeze"; "You're remembering to turn your body and eyes to the person who rang the bell"; "Everyone stayed frozen until I said 'You can melt.'"

It isn't necessary for all children to raise their hands when the teacher raises a hand. If the children get quiet when the teacher raises a hand or rings a chime or flicks the lights, then the signal is working. If some children want to help by also raising their hands (or copying whatever other hand signal that is used), that's great. But it's usually counterproductive to wait until every last child copies the signal before the teacher speaks.

Name expectations for group discussions

If students are going to be involved in the rule-creation process, or have group conversations of any substance, they'll need to learn guidelines for doing this well. Many teachers introduce what they call "meeting guidelines" or "conversation guidelines" during the first week of school.

These guidelines consist of four or five statements that name positive behavior expectations such as "Take turns"; "Raise your hand if you want to speak"; "Show respect for one another's ideas." The teacher can generate these guidelines alone or ask for students' input. The degree to which the teacher involves the children depends on the children's ability to take part in a productive discussion and on the teacher's comfort with facilitating a discussion like this early in the year.

If teachers decide to create the guidelines alone, it's important to write them as positive statements, naming expectations for children's positive behavior. When teachers present the guidelines to the children, they should link them to a purpose. For example, a teacher might say, "In our classroom, there'll be many times when we're having large group conversations. It's important that everyone participates in these conversations and that we all feel our ideas are heard. The following guidelines will help ensure that everyone can take part."

If teachers decide to work with the students to construct the guidelines, it's important to set clear, non-negotiable parameters for the task. For example, the guidelines must support the goals that everyone has an opportunity to participate in conversations and that all ideas are heard.

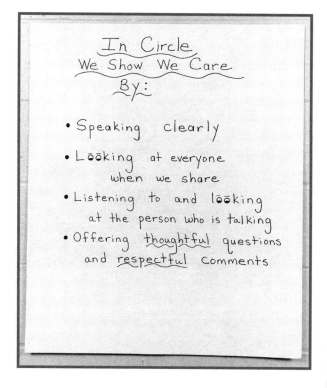

*Meeting guidelines in a first grade classroom (left)
and a fourth grade classroom (right).*

With these goals in mind, students will likely construct meeting guidelines that look very similar to what adults would create for their own meetings:

- Take turns.

- Raise your hand if you want to say something.

- Listen and show respect for each other's ideas.

If students frame a guideline in the negative such as "Don't talk when someone is speaking," the teacher asks them to reframe it in the positive: "So if we're not going to talk while others are speaking, what should we be doing?"

Also, if there are essential guidelines that the teacher feels are missing, he can add them. For example, a teacher might say, "I know that if I'm talking and people are moving their bodies a lot or waving their hands to get called on, I get distracted. I'd like to add two guidelines: 'Keep your body still when someone is talking' and 'Wait until the person is finished talking before raising your hand.'"

Once the list seems complete, the teacher, working alone or with students, can create a final list of four or five guidelines that are then posted in the group meeting area. The teacher can refer students to these guidelines during group conversations, especially during the early weeks of school: "Our guideline says that we should listen when someone is talking" or "Remember we said we'd raise our hands if we want to say something during a meeting."

Reflect on the purposes of rules

Why do we need rules in the classroom? For that matter, why do we need rules at all? While it seems a simple question with perhaps obvious answers, it's an essential one for teachers to ask themselves before inviting students into the process of articulating classroom rules.

Many of us have a love/hate relationship with rules. We know that rules are necessary for a well-functioning democracy and we wouldn't want to live in a lawless society, yet we sometimes get annoyed when we're told what to do.

Before discussing rules with students, it's important for teachers to examine their own feelings and assumptions about rules. If they're feeling ambivalent about the purpose of rules in the classroom, students will certainly pick up on these feelings.

Here are some questions to consider: What do you believe about the value of rules? What purpose do you think they serve? Take a few minutes to write down why you think rules are important in the classroom. Then, compare your list to the one on the next page.

Rules in the classroom:

- Create a sense of order and predictability

- Create a climate of respect

- Create a climate in which children feel safe enough to take risks

- Serve as guidelines for behavior to help children learn self-regulation

Begin the rule-creation process with "hopes and dreams"

During the first week of school, teachers using the rule-creation approach described in this book invite students to answer the important question, "What do you hope to learn and do this year in school?" While the question may seem simple, posing it to students and asking them to share their responses can have a profound effect on the classroom. Just think about the messages inherent in the question: What you care about matters at school; your hopes and goals are taken seriously here; you have a say in what you'll learn.

Taking the time to help students articulate their goals for school—or their "hopes and dreams" as they're often called—sets a tone of collaboration and mutual respect. It also fosters reflection and self-knowledge by prompting children to ask themselves questions such as "What's important to me at school? What do I want to get better at? What do I care about?"

Sharing individual goals for the school year creates a meaningful context for creating classroom rules. Once students have articulated their goals, the teacher asks, "If these are our hopes and dreams, what rules will we need so we can make all of these hopes and dreams come true?" In this way, rules become logical outgrowths of the students' and teachers' goals, something that will help them achieve their hopes, rather than directives handed down from above.

In order for this process to work, however, teachers must guide students toward thinking about goals that are realistic, learning-oriented, and achievable in school. It's not realistic for a child to "become a famous ballerina" or "become a basketball star" this year, for example. And "having recess all day" or "having lunch all day" is not related to the work of school. Here are essential ways to ensure that children name hopes and dreams that will be truly useful and meaningful:

Set the context by talking about the kinds of work done in classrooms

Before asking students what they hope to accomplish, primary grade teachers might give the children a tour of the classroom and talk about some of the things they'll be doing in school this coming year. Teachers of older children might ask students to think back on the previous year and name an accomplishment they felt proud of and something that was difficult for them.

Express your own goals for the school year

Many teachers express their own hopes for the students in the coming year before asking students to express theirs. This sets the tone and establishes clear expectations about the kinds of goals that students will be naming.

Part of a hopes and dreams display in a first grade classroom.

Although the teacher's language will vary depending on the age of the students, the point is to express a desire for a classroom that is safe, caring, and filled with learning.

For example, a second grade teacher might say, "This year I hope our classroom will be a safe and caring place to learn and that everyone will do their best work." A fifth grade teacher might say, "This year I hope that students can be friendly with everyone and learn how to work hard."

Use qualifiers when asking students to name their goals

Instead of asking "What do you hope to do this year?" teachers should ask, "What do you hope to learn in our classroom this year?" or "What do you hope you'll be able to work on in our classroom this year?" or "What are some social or academic skills you hope to work on this year in school?" Limiting the question to the arenas of work, learning, skills, classroom, and school helps make sure students name goals that will be attainable.

Below are some examples of how students at various grade levels expressed their goals when teachers used the process described above:

"I hope I get to build with the blocks and play a lot." KINDERGARTEN STUDENT

"I hope I get to do lots of hard work." FIRST GRADE STUDENT

"I hope to learn how to count money." SECOND GRADE STUDENT

"I hope to get better at math." THIRD GRADE STUDENT

"I hope I learn to spell better." FOURTH GRADE STUDENT

"I hope I'll make some new friends." FIFTH GRADE STUDENT

"I hope I do a lot of interesting projects." SIXTH GRADE STUDENT

"I hope to improve my grades and enjoy my classes." SEVENTH GRADE STUDENT

"I hope to be able to read better and faster and to get over my shyness." EIGHTH GRADE STUDENT

Have students share their goals

It's important that children share their goals with the class because the sharing helps students develop an awareness of and appreciation for one another's goals.

OUR HOPES & DREAMS

Kevin R. - My goal is to pass.

Eddie - to pass the 8th grade and to make new friends

Adam - to pass with at least straight B's.

Alyssa - to pass with good grades

Julie - to do all my homework and do good on tests

Stephanie - pass all of my classes and the MCAS tests

Katie - to stay focused and avoid distractions that keep me from performing to my fullest potential

Destiny - to remain on the Honor Society and to make the cheerleading team

Heather - to do all my homework

Aaron - to pass

Megan - to pass the 8th grade

Karina - to work hard and pass the 8th grade and to reach my destiny

Mrs. Cancelliéri - to help my students achieve their full potential and to have fun

Trevor - to pass the eigth GRADE

Frances - to not get in trouble and pass the 8th grade with at least a B average

Bianca - meet new people and get good grades

Shauntay - pass and work hard, pass MCAS, just enjoy being in eight grade

Mi ~ pass 8th grade, have good grades, pass MCAS, find new friends

Waheed - to do the best that I can do

Marissa - pass the 8th Grade with good grades

Kayla - get good grades

Sheng - pass 8th grade, have good grades, meet new people, get high honors, pass the MCAS test

Alex - pass the 8th grade

Kevin L. - pass the 8th grade

Meng - get the same grades as last year

Celeste - pass the 8th grade by getting good grades and staying out of trouble. And do my best to be a good student.

Chou - to pass and play for the school soccer team

Andrew - go to the high school and get good grades

Ray - to get good grades

C.J. - to have at least a B average + Get homework in on time

---

Our Hopes & Dreams for 3rd Grade

Angela hopes to be a better reader.
Nija hopes to learn cursive writing.
Kiana hopes to get better at math.
Jetor hopes to learn the multiplication tables.
Micah hopes to be a better reader.
Justin hopes to get good grades.
Ariela hopes to learn about the continents.
Caroline hopes to become a better speller.
Aldi hopes to learn more about history.
Yaser hopes to meet more teachers and friends.
Najauh hopes to get better at reading.
Adriana hopes to learn more about science.
Erick hopes to learn how to do division.
Daniel hopes to become a better artist.
Ashley hopes to be a better math student.
Julio hopes to learn how to write in cursive.
Omario hopes to learn a lot of new things.
Harrison hopes to make new friends.
Quinn hopes to get better at writing.
Juan hopes to do hard math.
Rene hopes to learn more about computers.
Daphne hopes to read long chapter books.
Mrs. W. hopes that all the students will learn to love books and reading.

Students' hopes and dreams are often displayed as simple lists.

How students share their goals varies depending on the age of the children and the teacher's style. Students might each draw pictures of what it would look like to achieve their individual goals, write in journals about their goals, or share their goals verbally in a small or large group. Below are some ways that teachers at different grade levels have structured the sharing of goals:

Kindergarten to second grade

- Children begin by sharing their many goals verbally. The teacher then asks each child to think about a most important hope for the year and to share this with the group. The teacher records these on a chart.

- Each child draws a picture representing his or her most important hope for the year, and the teacher (or the children themselves if they are able) records the children's words on the pictures. These can be displayed immediately as a "Hopes and Dreams" bulletin board or later as part of the display on classroom rules.

- Each child draws a picture of achieving a most important goal and then shares the picture with a partner. Children then report back to the group about their partners' goals. Or, if the teacher has a digital camera, students could pose for photos depicting what it would look like to accomplish their goals.

A third grader's hope and dream illustration. "I hope to be a better reader and get to level Q in reading."

Third to fifth grade

- After an initial conversation about hopes for the year, students write in journals to express their many goals for the school year. The next day they reread these journal entries and each child decides on one most important hope for the school year to share with the class.

- Using drawing, collage, or photography, each student illustrates a most important hope for the school year. Children share these with the group and then the illustrations are mounted and displayed in the classroom or hallway.

Sixth to eighth grade

- Students write in journals at school or as a homework assignment, reflecting on the previous year of school and articulating their hopes, dreams, and worries for this year. One possible structure for reflecting on the previous year is for students to think about things they felt successful at, things they didn't feel successful at, things they loved to do, and things they dreaded doing. Each chooses one item from each category to journal about.

- As a whole class, students brainstorm possible goals in different categories: a social goal, an academic goal, an athletic goal, etc. With this to get them thinking, students then write about their own goals in these categories and choose three or four goals, each from a different category, to share with the group. This allows students to express more than one goal for the year, something children this age often like to do.

After goals have been named and shared, they are displayed prominently in the room. The teacher can then begin a conversation about classroom rules by referring to everyone's goals. The display reinforces the idea that classroom rules grow out of everyone's goals for the year.

Invite families into the process

Many teachers invite families into this process of articulating goals for the year. There's no question that families are more likely to trust and support this approach to discipline if they understand the thinking behind it. Inviting families to express their own hopes for their child is a good first step to building this important sense of trust. Here are a few possible ways to do this:

- At the first family–teacher conference (preferably before the first day of school), share your hopes for the year. Then ask the family to share theirs: "What are your most important hopes for your child in school this year?" or "What do you think is most important for your child to learn in school this year?" It's best to send this question to families ahead of time so they can think about it before the conference.

- Early in the school year, send a letter to families explaining the process of establishing goals and inviting them to write back with their goals for their child this year. Some teachers ask families specifically to share an academic goal and a social goal. Others leave the question more open-ended.

- In preparation for the first open house, create a "Hopes and Dreams" display showing all of the students' goals for the year. Students can write personal letters to their families asking them to share their most important hopes for the school year.

Generate a list of preliminary rules

"If these are our hopes and dreams, what rules will we need to help us make them come true?" This is a pivotal question and one that teachers ask soon after students have articulated their hopes for the year. Thinking through this question helps students make the important connection between their personal hopes for the year and the classroom rules.

It also helps them to see that everyone's learning goals are important and that the rules are there to help everyone succeed. Without these understandings, the rules will hold little meaning.

There are various ways to begin the process of generating rules. Some teachers begin with a whole-group discussion: "If Tai wants to get better at writing and Evalina to learn Spanish and Sheng to learn how to do division, what rules will we need to help them reach these goals? What rules will we need to help all of us reach our goals? Let's start by making a list."

Other teachers, especially those of upper grades, prefer to have students begin by reflecting personally and writing about classroom rules. They might begin: "If these are our goals for the year, what do you think will be the one to three most important rules for our class?" For homework or as an in-class writing assignment, students then name the rules and explain why they think those are the most important ones.

To help older students feel freer and more honest with this assignment, teachers can assure students that their responses will be kept confidential. Once the writings are complete, the teacher can assemble a list of proposed rules for discussion, perhaps noting how often each rule appeared in students' writings but without attaching names to the rules.

Help students frame the rules in the positive

Regardless of how a teacher goes about this initial task of generating rules with students, it's likely that many of the rules will be expressed in the negative, a clue, perhaps, to how children generally perceive rules in our society. For example, here's part of a first attempt at a list of rules from a third grade class:

Do not scare or yell at anyone.

Don't be rude.

Don't lie to the teacher.

Don't fight in line.

No fighting at recess.

The task now is to help students reframe the rules in the positive. One way to do this is to stop every time a negative rule is expressed and ask students to try to reframe it in the positive. For example, when a child suggests, "Do not scare or yell at anyone," the teacher can say, "We don't want to scare or yell at anyone here. So if we're not going to scare or yell at anyone, how do you think we should treat or talk to each other?" Some responses from students might include:

"Talk to others in a respectful way."

"Use a friendly voice."

"Stay in control even if you're mad."

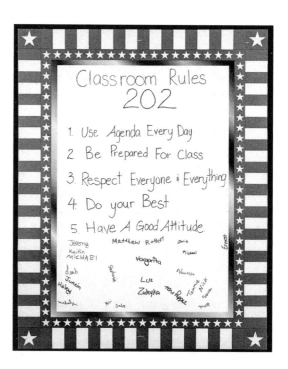

Our 8th Grade Class Rules

1. Treat others the way you want them and expect them to treat you.
2. Pay attention and talk on your own time.
3. Be prepared for class.
4. Respect other people's property.
5. Be organized and take care of all materials and our environment.

Classroom Rules 202

1. Use Agenda Every Day
2. Be Prepared For Class
3. Respect Everyone & Everything
4. Do your Best
5. Have A Good Attitude.

Jeremy   Matthew Robert   Chris   Ernest   Kaitlin   MICHAEL   Michael   Harprita   Leah   Stephanie   Nancessa   Junain   Luz   Peter Peppi   Tommie Nick Conor   Haley   Zuleyka   Madelyn   Khi Jady   Trick

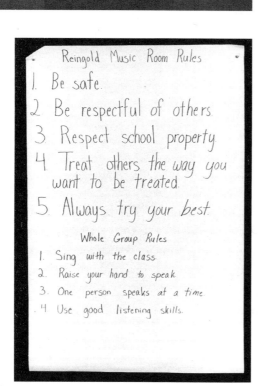

Reingold Music Room Rules

1. Be safe.
2. Be respectful of others.
3. Respect school property.
4. Treat others the way you want to be treated.
5. Always try your best.

Whole Group Rules

1. Sing with the class.
2. Raise your hand to speak.
3. One person speaks at a time.
4. Use good listening skills.

Classroom rules can be displayed in a variety of styles, depending on the children's age and preference.

CLASSROOM RULES

- Be kind, caring, and helpful to each other.
- Take care of classroom materials.
- Show respect for others.

Sarah   Max Harmon   Michael Garcia   Alison   Max Vandale   Jonathan   Angelica   Richard   Paul   Michaela   Amanda   Erik Danial   Nicole   Sarah   Natasha   Shaquille   miguel   Nick   Anna Mae Schley   Chris A   RYAN

Another possibility is to complete the entire list and then change the negative rules into positive ones. The teacher might say, "There are lots of rules here that tell us what not to do. It's more helpful to have rules that tell us what to do. Let's see if we can say those rules in a different way so they will help us know what to do."

Thus in the third grade class mentioned above, "Do not scare or yell at anyone" became "Talk to others in a respectful way." "Don't be rude" became "Think about other people's feelings." "Don't lie to the teacher" became "Tell the truth" (here the teacher also helped children realize it's important to be honest not just with the teacher, but with everyone). "Don't fight in line" became "Keep your hands to yourself and be quiet when you're in line," and so forth.

It takes some work to get children to turn their don'ts into dos. But it's important work because our goal is to give children guidelines for positive behavior. By framing the rules in the positive, we shift the emphasis from rules that foster compliance to rules that foster self-control and a sense of responsibility to a group. They are constant reminders of what everyone in the classroom, including the teachers, is striving to become. They represent our community ideals.

From the long list of positive rules, create a few global ones

Remember the third grader in the introduction who expressed her relief that in her school "there isn't too many rules" but "just a few good ones"? Both teachers and students will feel this same relief when they can consolidate their long list of rules into "a few good ones." Long lists of rules, even when expressed in the positive, are simply too overwhelming to be truly useful.

A long list of specific rules also becomes a prescriptive recipe. A short list of broad rules, on the other hand, fosters ethical thinking and the practice of self-regulation by giving children the opportunity to apply general behavior expectations to a range of situations.

While students might have generated a list of twenty to thirty possible rules in the first round of discussions, the teacher can now help them see that most of these rules will fall into three to five general categories. The categories that teachers typically use are:

- Taking care of ourselves

- Taking care of others

- Taking care of our classroom and materials

- Taking care to do our best work

The teacher might begin the consolidation process by saying, "This is a great list of rules, but there are so many of them. I know that I won't be able to remember all these rules. I wonder if we can put some of them together so that we only have a few rules to remember." Or, for older students, "This is a good list to start with, but I'm noticing that lots of these rules overlap each other. How could we group them so that we have just a few rules for our class?"

For younger students, the teacher might suggest exactly what the three to five sorting categories will be: "Let's see if each of these rules will fit under one of these categories: taking care of ourselves, taking care of others, taking care of our classroom, and doing our best work."

In upper grades, the teacher might invite students, perhaps working in pairs, to determine what the three to five sorting categories will be. In all likelihood, the categories they come up with will be very similar to the ones stated above: care for ourselves, care for others, care for materials, and care for our work. But the process of sorting and synthesizing takes the students to a depth of understanding—of the meaning of the rules and of each other—that may not otherwise be possible.

When all the rules have been sorted into three to five categories, the class might want to adjust the wording of the categories. It is always illuminating to hear which words students choose to use—their words are a clue to what they really understand the rules to mean. And because their words are a way for students to communicate nuances of understanding to each other, it's appropriate to let students spend some time on wordsmithing. That said, keep in mind that the exact wording of the final rules is less important than the process of getting to them. Try not to let the class, especially if it's a group of passionate debaters, get too hung up on the details of the wording.

Here are a few examples of the final list of rules—global, positive, and few in number—from several classrooms:

From a second grade classroom

- Take care of yourself and keep everybody safe.

- Help and respect other people.

- Be gentle and take care of all the things in our school.

- Try your hardest and do your best work.

From a fourth grade classroom

- Be in control of yourself.

- Be helpful and respectful of others.

- Treat people the way you want to be treated.

- Be a thinking worker.

From an eighth grade classroom

- Cooperate with each other.

- Listen to each other.

- Take care of our classroom and school environment.

- Show respect for others and their materials.

Talk about what the Golden Rule really means

Often children come up with some version of the Golden Rule—"Treat others as you'd like to be treated"—as one of their classroom rules. While this is an accepted tenet that is present in many traditions, it can be confusing for children.

Young children, and even many older children, may take this saying literally. A literal understanding works in many situations: "If I want the people at this table to share the markers with me, I have to share the markers with them." But in many situations, it doesn't work: "If I don't mind when people kid me about my clothes, then it's okay for me to kid others about their clothes."

For this reason, many teachers whose students come up with this rule make it a point to discuss what the Golden Rule really means. They help students understand that the rule is about the broad idea of treating others with respect and care, just as the students themselves would like to be treated with respect and care. Part of living by the rule is learning what respect and care look like, sound like, and feel like to the other person rather than using ourselves as the standard. With this understanding, children will be more able to make sense of the Golden Rule and use it in their everyday school life.

Celebrate and share the rules

After working so hard to create this final list of rules that will become the cornerstone of classroom life, it's fitting for the class to celebrate these rules and share them with students' families. Here are a few ideas that teachers have used:

Send a letter home to families

In the letter, celebrate the classroom rules and ask for family support. (See the sample letter on page 41.)

Have students make a beautiful display of the rules

Perhaps they can write the final rules on a large piece of poster board and surround it with illustrations. In some classes, all students sign the poster to show that they agree to try to live by the rules. Display the poster in a prominent place in the room.

Dear Families,

We have been talking a lot during these early weeks of school about our learning goals for this school year. The students and I have articulated many goals for ourselves. Here's a list of our most important ones:

[List the students' and teacher's most important hopes for the year.]

To create a climate where all students can achieve their goals, we have created the following rules for our classroom:

[List the rules that the students and teacher have created.]

You can help us at home. Please keep these lists in a prominent place and refer to the rules often with your child. We are all working together to create a safe and caring community of learners. I appreciate your support. Please feel free to call me if you have questions about these rules or my approach to classroom discipline.

Sincerely,

So, are classrooms that use this process of rule creation more lax than those using an autocratic approach? This is a common question. The answer is absolutely not. Just because the rules are stated in the positive and students are involved in creating them doesn't mean that behavior expectations are in any way "fuzzy" or lower than in other classrooms.

On the contrary, behavior expectations are high as teachers strive to be firm, clear, and consistent. Both teachers and students are highly invested in the rules, and both serve as caretakers of them. Children value the rules more when the rules are their own.

When the Teacher Creates the Rules

There might be times when it makes sense for the teacher to take sole responsibility for creating the rules. For example:

- Your school or district expects teachers to present rules at the very beginning of the year.

- Past experience says that the children in your classroom will need the clear boundaries of classroom rules in place on day one.

- You aren't sure the children will have the skills necessary to engage in meaningful discussions about rules.

- You are not comfortable with the idea of facilitating these discussions with children.

Provide a structure for thinking about and sharing goals

Even if you are creating the rules yourself, it's important to talk with students about their goals for the year. The timing of when you have these conversations will vary: You will want to be sure that children feel safe enough in the classroom and positive enough about school to engage in a meaningful discussion about goals. And you might not go through every step in the process described on pages 28–34. Instead, choose those steps that you think children in your classroom can engage in most productively.

Create rules that are global, few in number, positively stated

Following are some tips to help you create meaningful classroom rules:

- It could be a helpful exercise to follow the steps described for collaborative rule-making (considering goals, writing a long list of specific rules, restating them in the positive, grouping them into categories) when you create your own rules.

- If your school has schoolwide rules in place, think about how you might adapt them to meet your classroom goals and needs.

- Begin with rules you've put in place in years past and adapt for the needs of this year's students.

Once you've got a draft list of rules, pay attention to the wording. Have you stated the rules positively? Have you phrased things in a way that children will understand? Although we want the rules to be global, we also want them to be understandable and relevant to children.

Connect the rules to everyone's goals

Children will be most likely to accept the rules if they can see a connection between the rules and their own classroom goals:

- If you've had a discussion with children about their goals for the year, use this information when you create rules. When you present the rules, be sure to talk with children about how the rules will help them achieve their goals.

- Follow a discussion about goals with a discussion about what rules might help children achieve those goals. Use the information you learn from that discussion to create the final list of rules yourself.

- If you establish rules on day one, choose a time later in the year to engage in a modified version of the collaborative process to amend the initial rules.

Review: Establishing Safety, Identifying Goals, and Creating Rules

1. Consider which routines are essential to classroom safety.

2. Plan how to introduce these routines in the first days of school.

3. Use interactive modeling to teach and practice key routines, such as responding to a signal for quiet.

4. Establish expectations for group discussions.

5. Work with students to identify their individual goals.

6. Create a list of rules that help students meet their learning goals.

WORKS CITED

Damon, William. (1999, August). The Moral Development of the Child. *Scientific American*, 56–62.

Denton, Paula, and Kriete, Roxann. (2000). *The First Six Weeks of School.* Greenfield, MA: Northeast Foundation for Children, Inc.

Teaching Positive Behavior: Bringing the Rules to Life

Purposes and Reflections

Establishing classroom rules and behavior expectations is a good starting point for positive behavior. But just because children can articulate the rules doesn't mean they will follow them. Controlling impulses, expressing feelings in a constructive way, and putting personal needs aside momentarily for the good of the group are complex, demanding skills—skills that even adults struggle with. I don't need to think hard to remember the last time I interrupted someone who was speaking even though I knew it was rude. I often break the speed limit even though I know it isn't safe or legal. More often than I'd like to admit, I raise my voice even though I know I'm acting out of anger.

If living by accepted codes of behavior and rules is challenging for adults, it can be even harder for children. Children in elementary school are just beginning to learn self-control, communication skills, perspective taking, and the myriad other skills needed to live and learn peacefully with others. Chip Wood, author and educational consultant, says, "Children need opportunities, under the caring guidance and support of adults, to practice these essential skills, over and over again, without criticism and judgment." (Wood, 1998)

To be successful, children need lots of encouragement, support, and practice. And they need adults who celebrate improvement, rather than demand perfection. Our job as teachers is to help children understand what it means to do the right thing, give them opportunities to practice positive behaviors, and offer support along the way.

The goals of practicing positive behavior with students, then, are to:

- Further students' understanding of behavior expectations

- Help students understand how general expectations (e.g., be respectful) translate into concrete actions

- Establish clear and specific behavior expectations for various settings (reading groups, meeting area, recess, when there's a guest teacher, etc.)

- Encourage ethical thinking and internalization of the rules

Getting Started

During the first few months of school, but most intensively during the early weeks, it's essential to make global behavior expectations real and concrete by applying them to different classroom situations. This is not a step-by-step or finite process. Instead, it is done continuously throughout the year, as part of planned lessons and in the moment as needed.

Strategies that teachers might use to make behavior expectations concrete and teach positive behavior, using the classroom rules as guideposts, include:

- *Structured discussion* to help children apply general guidelines to specific situations

- *Interactive modeling* to teach and rehearse appropriate behaviors in situations where there is one way to do something

- *Role-playing* to help students prepare for situations where there is more than one way to do something

- *Teacher language* to reinforce, remind, and redirect students as they apply the rules to their daily lives

Structured discussion: Discuss specific application of general expectations

"Our rules say we will respect each other. What will that look like and sound like when we're in reading groups today?" If we want children to think for themselves and learn to make ethical decisions about their behavior, we need to help them visualize the actions and words that constitute positive behavior.

A powerful way to do this is through discussion of how the rules apply to specific situations. These discussions don't need to be long or weighty. In fact, it's best if they are brief and immediate, closely linked in time to the activity or situation.

For example, in preparing children for recess, a teacher might say, "Our rules say that we will take care of each other and keep people safe. What's one thing you'll do to keep your classmates safe when you're on the playground today?" The students might respond, "Tag gently"; "Help someone if they fall down"; "Let everyone play."

Discussions can also happen after an event to help students reflect on their behavior. For example, after recess the teacher might ask: "What was the hardest rule to follow during recess today? What could we do better next time?" Frequent short discussions like these help children make important connections between behavior expectations and their actions.

Use open-ended questions to get discussions started

Open-ended questions are those for which there is no one right or wrong answer. Instead, any reasoned and relevant answer is correct. Open-ended questions can spark useful discussions because they challenge students to think deeply about a situation, draw on prior knowledge, and listen carefully to one another's ideas.

Here are some tips for asking good open-ended questions:

Be clear about what you're asking for. A question such as "How did we do during recess?" might be too general for most children to respond to easily. Instead, clarify that you want them to think about which rules were easy or difficult to follow.

Be genuinely curious. If you ask a question with an idea in mind about how children should answer, they'll know that you're not really interested in hearing their responses. Instead, cultivate genuine curiosity about children's thinking—and only open these discussions when you are interested in hearing children's thoughts.

Watch out for pseudo open-ended questions. If you use the structure and language of open-ended questions but have an idea in mind of how children should answer, the question won't be truly open-ended.

(For more information about open-ended questions, please see *The Power of Our Words* by Paula Denton, EdD.)

Pay attention to the timing of the discussion and structure carefully

The timing and structure of these discussions will vary depending on children's age and their ability to think reflectively about their behavior. With young children or children who have little experience reflecting on behavior, teachers will want to start small and structure the discussions carefully. For example, teachers might focus on one question, using language that relates to children's daily lives. When wiggliness starts to take over, it's time to stop the discussion. Meeting rules posted in the circle area can remind the children of the basic procedures and expectations during discussion time (see Chapter One). With older children, who might have a more sophisticated ability to reflect on behavior and feelings, these discussions can be more wide-ranging.

At any age, a useful strategy for structuring the discussion is the T-chart, which provides a concrete structure to help children apply abstract rules to specific situations. A teacher might ask, "What would our rule to take care of our classroom environment look like during choice time? What would it sound like?" As children give their responses, the teacher fills in the appropriate columns on the chart, which then gets posted for ongoing reference.

Take care of our classroom during choice time	
Looks like	Sounds like

Here is an example of a basic T-chart structure.

Interactive modeling: Use modeling to teach and practice routine behaviors

Interactive modeling is a strategy that is used at the beginning of the year to help teach important routines (see Chapter One). Modeling might be used, for example, to teach how to pass materials to someone, what to do while waiting in line, how to carry scissors, and how to show that you're listening. It is also used throughout the year to learn new routines and revisit routines and behaviors learned in the first days of school.

Modeling doesn't need to be a time-consuming process. It can be brief and happen spontaneously throughout the day, especially when it is used

Steps in Interactive Modeling

1. *Describe the positive behavior to be modeled.*

2. *Demonstrate the behavior.*

3. *Ask students what they noticed about the demonstrated behavior.*

4. *Ask student volunteers to demonstrate the same behavior.*

5. *Ask students what they noticed.*

6. *Students practice; teacher observes and coaches, using reinforcing language.*

as a refresher. Although using all six modeling steps is the most effective way to teach new routines, teachers will sometimes choose to skip one of the steps, especially when they are revisiting previously taught and modeled routines.

For example, Ms. T. has observed that her third grade students have been getting a bit sloppy about putting away their reading materials. She decides to do a quick re-modeling of the routine she taught in the first week of school. Since she knows that the students know how to do this routine, she decides to skip the step of the teacher modeling.

Right before lunchtime, she rings the bell and tells students that it's time to put away reading materials. She asks, "Who can remind us how to put away our reading materials in a safe and careful way?"

"You should walk."

"Put all the papers back in the folder neatly. Don't just shove them in there."

"Wait for your turn if someone's in front of you. Don't push."

"Great," says Ms. T. "You're remembering our rules about taking care of each other and our materials. Who would like to show us?"

Three children raise their hands. As the rest of the students watch from their seats, the three volunteers follow the suggestions given by their classmates. They put their papers away neatly in the folder, walk to the file cabinet, put their folders away, and line up at the door.

"What did you notice?" asks Ms. T.

"Dwayne had to take all his papers out to get them in neatly."

"Thea waited for Helen to finish 'cause their files were right next to each other."

"They all walked. No one bumped into each other."

"It was really quiet."

"Okay, now everyone can put away reading folders and line up for lunch," Ms. T. says.

Modeling can also be fun. Anything involving acting is inherently fun for children. Students enjoy being the one "onstage" as well as watching others in this role. It's important to recognize and keep hold of the playfulness of this technique. Done in too somber or heavy-handed a way, the technique of modeling will quickly lose its appeal and effectiveness.

The teacher as constant modeler: Children are always watching

When it comes to classroom rules, the adage "Children do as we do, not as we say" couldn't be more true. They learn just as much—if not more—from our spontaneous interactions as they do from our deliberate lessons. That's why it's so important to pay attention to our own behavior, in all our interactions with children and adults.

Easier said than done, of course. How many of us have heard ourselves yell at a child, "Do not raise your voice when you talk to me!"? Or speak to a student in a sarcastic or threatening way? Or be dismissive of a parent offering a suggestion for a problem? Just like children, when we're frustrated or angry, tired or stressed, we often lose control of ourselves and forget or ignore the rules. Knowing that we're doing it is often not enough to make us stop.

The point here is not to be perfect. We all know that's impossible. The point is to keep in mind that students are watching at all times, to try to follow the classroom rules whenever possible, and to acknowledge any mistakes we make.

A simple "I'm sorry I yelled yesterday. I was feeling angry and I forgot our rule about treating others the way we want to be treated" is all that's needed. This sends the message that the rules are important—even the teacher tries her best to follow them—and that everyone makes mistakes. It says that we're all learners here and we don't have to be ashamed of our mistakes.

Role-play: Use role-playing to prepare children for more complex situations

Role-playing helps students prepare for complex social interactions that require them to choose from among a range of possible positive behaviors. The teacher and students discuss the situations, brainstorm possible ways to handle them, and then act them out. For example, a teacher might use role-playing to help students think about how to include someone in an activity, how to be a good sport when you're winning or losing a game, and what to do when you disagree with your partner's ideas. Role-playing allows teachers to acknowledge the complexity of these situations and give students practice in making responsible choices.

Choosing and framing role-playing situations

Role-plays are generally done with the whole class but can also be done with small groups or even with an individual child. It's best if the role-playing situations spring from the life of the classroom. For example, the teacher may know from prior experience that students are likely to:

- Have difficulty sharing materials

- Laugh at or show intolerance for one another's mistakes

- Become inflamed over accidents such as someone knocking something over, taking something another student is still using, or bumping into someone else

- Exclude certain students

- Interrupt when someone is speaking

The teacher chooses one issue at a time to address through role-playing. Before launching into the process, the teacher reframes the problem in positive terms. The list of problems above might be reframed in the following ways:

- "Students have difficulty sharing materials" might become "We need to work on sharing our supplies."

- "Students laugh at one another's mistakes" might be reframed as "We need to work on being supportive of one another, especially when someone makes a mistake."

- "Students become inflamed over accidents" might become "We need to work on staying calm when someone does something by accident."

Steps in a role-play

Once the teacher has established the positive goal of the role-play, students and teachers work collaboratively to name and act out possible behaviors. While the goal itself is never negotiable—for example, deciding not to be inclusive is not an option—there can be several routes to achieving that goal. After seeing several possible solutions enacted, students will have an expanded repertoire of behavior choices when faced with the real-life situation.

Following are the steps typically used in a role-play, along with examples of each step:

1. **Describe the scenario.** The teacher describes the situation to be role-played using language that will make the scene come to life for the students and engage them in the role-play. One way to do this is to use first-person narration from a student's point of view. Stop the narration just before the point where a behavior decision—and possible conflict—will occur.

   > *"Imagine that it's sharing time and a classmate, we'll call her Jessica, begins to share about seeing the most recent Harry Potter movie. I love Harry Potter and have seen the movie three times. I think I know every line. I'm so excited—I want to tell someone about my favorite scene but I know I need to listen to Jessica."*

2. **Name the positive goal.** The teacher describes the positive goal, connecting it to the classroom rules.

   > *"Our classroom rule says, 'Respect each other.' How can I be a respectful listener when I'm really eager to say something myself?"*

3. *Invite and chart students' ideas.* The teacher invites the students to brainstorm ideas for how to behave in the situation that was described. The students call out possible behavior strategies while the teacher charts their ideas. It's important to make sure the strategies are framed positively.

> *Students think for a minute and then begin to call out ideas: "You need to sit quietly until Jessica's finished, but I bet you'll look really interested!"*
>
> *"When Jessica's done you could ask her a question."*
>
> *"I know we're not supposed to make 'me, too' comments during sharing but you could go up to Jessica later and tell her you really liked the movie too. Maybe the two of you could talk about it during lunch."*

4. *Role-play one of the suggestions, with the teacher in the lead role.* It's important that the teacher take the lead role at first in order to maintain control of the tone of the role-play. During the role-play, the audience notices actions, feelings, voice tone, and words used.

> *The teacher asks for a student volunteer to play the role of Jessica and takes a few minutes to coach the volunteer and help her think of what she might say. When the role-play begins, the teacher sits with a really erect, alert posture and a big smile while listening to "Jessica's" sharing.*

5. *Ask students what they noticed.* The teacher asks students in the audience to share their observations.

> *After the role-play, student observers share that the teacher sat up straight, looked "Jessica" in the eye, and looked excited about what "Jessica" was saying but didn't try to interrupt.*

6. *Act out other suggestions in the list.* Choose new actors and replay the scene using another suggestion. If the teacher thinks students are ready, they can take all the roles, including the lead role. Again, audience members observe actions, feelings, voice tone, and words and share their observations at the end of the scene.

Teacher language: Use reinforcing, reminding, and redirecting language

Research has shown over and over that children's academic performance is influenced both positively and negatively by teachers' expectations. If a teacher believes a child will succeed, the child has a greater chance of doing so than if the teacher believes the child will fail.

The same holds true for children's behavior. Most children will try to live up to adult expectations. If we expect that children will be respectful and responsible, they will strive to be. If we expect that children will be disrespectful and irresponsible, then that's what they most likely will be.

Teacher language is one key way through which we communicate our expectations to children. Through our language we let children know that we have confidence in their ability to meet high expectations—and that we recognize their efforts at positive behavior. Our language encourages and supports students, rather than criticizing them for their mistakes. As child psychologist Rudolf Dreikurs writes, "Each child needs continuous encouragement just as a plant needs water." (Dreikurs, 1964, p. 36)

The teacher language used in the *Responsive Classroom* approach falls into three general categories—reinforcing, reminding, and redirecting language.

Reinforcing language

Reinforcing language names and affirms children's positive behaviors. Recognizing that children build on their strengths, teachers use reinforcing language to help children know exactly what they are doing well and to help them grow academically and socially.

Following are examples of reinforcing language:

- "Vinnie, you offered to help Emelyne clean the table. That's an important way of taking care of our classroom."

- "What a smooth cleanup that was. You put away your math work, got your lunches, lined up for music, and talked to each other calmly when you needed someone to move over and let you get by."

Three Kinds of Teacher Language

	Reinforcing	Reminding	Redirecting
When to use	When the teacher notices efforts at self-discipline	■ Before students start an activity or enter into a situation ■ Just as students begin to show inappropriate behavior	When students have clearly gone off course and are definitely showing inappropriate behavior
How to use	Acknowledge positive actions by naming them.	Give students a chance to name or show an appropriate alternative behavior.	Stop the behavior and tell the child what to do instead.
Example	"You're all asking relevant questions and making supportive comments."	"Show me how we agreed to share these materials."	"Stop. We walk in the halls."

■ "Jenelle, you were working on using friendly words at the art table this morning. I think your classmates noticed too."

■ "You used lots of descriptive language in your story about the visit to the farm. I got a clear picture of all the animals you saw."

■ "You listened so carefully and attentively during sharing. Your questions and comments show that you're really paying attention to the speaker."

- "Tyesha, you worked hard on your math problems. When you didn't know an answer, you tried different strategies or asked a buddy for help."

Here are a few tips for using reinforcing language effectively:

NAME CONCRETE, SPECIFIC BEHAVIORS AND EMPHASIZE DESCRIPTION OVER PERSONAL APPROVAL

Teachers use reinforcing language to let children know exactly which aspects of their behavior or work the teacher is recognizing. However, it's important to do this in a way that stays focused on the children rather than on the teacher's approval. "Did you notice how quickly everyone cleaned up today?" is more effective than "I liked how you all cleaned up so quickly." The goal is to help children learn to self-assess and to increase children's internal sense of self-worth rather than having children always look to the teacher for validation.

Upper elementary teacher Kathryn Brady says that she avoids global judgments when she wants to acknowledge positive behavior, preferring to name specific behaviors. She says, "Sure, we want children to follow rules for many reasons, and sometimes the reasons include pleasing adults, but the most important reason for following rules is to allow the child or others in the class to achieve a positive goal. If I direct children's focus too often to my pleasure or displeasure by using global praise such as 'Good job,' I muddy the waters. If I name specific behaviors I'm keeping the focus on the children and the positive impact of their actions."

FIND POSITIVES TO NAME IN ALL STUDENTS

It's important that reinforcing language be used authentically with all children, not just those who excel. Teachers need to observe children carefully and acknowledge the small but important steps that children take towards mastery of a skill or behavior.

AVOID NAMING INDIVIDUALS AS EXAMPLES FOR OTHERS

It's tempting to hold one student's exemplary behavior up as a model for all students, but there are risks in doing so. The individual student might feel manipulated or distrustful of the teacher's positive feedback and the other students might feel resentful of the student. It's best to give individual reinforcement privately and to find more direct ways of letting students know what your expectations are.

BE SINCERE

While there may be a period of time when our language sounds a bit wooden because of changes we're trying to make in how we talk with children, it's important to always maintain our sincerity. Students know when our language is coming from a genuine place and when it's not. We're most effective as teachers when we're being authentic.

A WORD ABOUT PRAISE

Praise vs. encouragement is a debate that has persisted for many years among teachers, researchers, psychologists, and parents. There is mounting evidence that excessive use of general praise has negative consequences.

While praising students may seem to improve their behavior in the short term, it doesn't necessarily have long-term benefits. In a *New York Times* article on this topic, child-rearing experts cautioned that a steady stream of praise can turn children into praise addicts who lack confidence and who feel manipulated. (Belluck, 2000)

Po Bronson and Ashley Merryman, in their book *Nurture Shock* (2009), also caution against overuse and misuse of praise. Praise *can* be effective, they write, as long as it's specific and sincere. (pp. 19–20) Excessive praise, however, can undermine children's motivation to learn. They cite a meta-analysis done by scholars from Reed College and Stanford University which determined that "praised students became risk-aversive and lack perceived autonomy. . . . When they get to college, heavily praised students commonly drop out of classes rather than suffer a mediocre grade and they have a hard time picking a major—they're afraid to commit to something because they're afraid of not succeeding." (p. 21)

So does this mean that teachers should stop recognizing children's positive efforts and accomplishments? Absolutely not! Children, like all of us,

need to feel recognized for their positive contributions and accomplishments. And they need ongoing information from the teacher about how they're doing with regard to classroom behavior. What this caution about praise does mean is that teachers should be mindful of how they give this feedback.

There is still a place for genuine, celebratory praise. But if the goal is to help children become self-motivated and feel good inside about their own behavior, teachers might more often give feedback that is specific and encourages children to evaluate their own work or behavior.

Here are three tips for giving encouraging feedback:

- Comment on the specifics, especially something that you know the child is working hard on: "Carl, you looked at Eva the whole time while she was sharing her story today."

- Point out the positive benefits of the behavior: "Carl, you were really concentrating on Eva's sharing today. I bet that made her feel good."

- Ask questions in a way that shows interest, yet allows the child to judge him/herself: "You were paying attention during Eva's sharing today. How do you think Eva felt?"

FOCUSING ON WHAT'S BEHIND YOUR WORDS

All this said, it's important to note that getting too rigid about the sometimes subtle distinctions between praise and encouragement can be counterproductive. Rather than focusing hard on whether our words are technically considered praise or encouragement, it's better to focus on the intention behind our words.

If we're using language to manipulate or control, or if we're noticing that students are highly dependent on our positive feedback, then something probably needs to change. On the other hand, if we're using language to make meaningful connections with students, to give positive feedback, and to recognize specific accomplishments, then it probably will serve those purposes. While it's worthwhile to explore our choice of words, it may not be essential to change every expression.

Jane Nelsen, in her book *Positive Discipline*, offers the following questions to keep in mind when considering whether a statement is considered praise or encouragement:

- Am I inspiring self-evaluation or cultivating dependence on others' evaluation?

- Am I being respectful or patronizing?

- Am I seeing the child's point of view or only my own?

- Would I make this comment to a friend?

Teachers often find this last question especially useful. As Nelsen points out, "The comments we make to friends usually fit the criteria for encouragement." (Nelsen, 1996, pp. 120, 122)

Reminding language

Reminding language prompts children to remember established expectations and to make decisions about their actions based on those expectations. It communicates a teacher's trust in students' good intentions. Reminders can be either a question ("What are you supposed to be doing right now?") or a statement ("Show me how you should be doing this."). Unlike the "reminders" of day-to-day life, reminding language puts the responsibility for doing "the remembering" on the child rather than the adult who is doing the reminding.

Following are examples of reminding language:

- Before students start on a project that requires them to share markers, the teacher says, "Who can show us how to ask for a marker?" and then, "Who can show us how to pass a marker?"

- A group of students begins to fidget instead of doing their math work. They look like they're about to start fooling around with each other.

The teacher says, "What are you supposed to be doing right now? Show me."

- Before student presentations, the teacher says, "One of our rules says to respect each other. What do we need to do to be a respectful audience?"

- The teacher is about to release the children to independent work groups. During this time, small groups of children will rotate through the snack area. The teacher asks, "What do we need to remember to do at snack table so that other groups can do their best learning?"

- The teacher rings the chime to tell students they have five minutes left of their work period before cleanup time. "You have five minutes until cleanup. Think about what you need to do to be ready for cleanup."

Reminding language can be used effectively in two situations. First, it is used to help children prepare for an activity or situation. "Who remembers the three things we all need to have on our desks to be ready for dictation?" a teacher might say. This sets the children up for success. It can also be a genuine check-in that informs the teacher—and reassures the students— about the students' readiness to handle the situation.

Second, reminding language is used to steady the course when students are beginning to go off track. For example, just as the noise level in the room begins to rise, the teacher says, "Who remembers what we said about our voices during quiet time?"

Here are a few tips for using reminding language effectively:

ESTABLISH EXPECTATIONS BEFORE USING REMINDERS

In order to use reminders successfully, teachers need to teach and practice the routines and behavior expectations that the reminders refer to. Structured discussions (pp. 49–51) and interactive modeling (pp. 51–54) are two ways teachers can do this.

USE A DIRECT TONE AND NEUTRAL BODY LANGUAGE

Tone and body language communicate a lot about a teacher's underlying beliefs. No matter how carefully a teacher chooses her words, if her tone and body language convey impatience, irritation, or judgment, the message will be that she doesn't really have faith in children's good intentions. Reminders given in a direct tone with neutral body language are more likely to be heard as helpful cues.

KEEP REMINDERS BRIEF

Children are masterful at tuning out adults, especially those who go on and on. Remember the old Charlie Brown cartoons, in which the adults' words droned on in a long series of blah, blah, blahs? Using too many words confuses and overwhelms children. After a certain point, they stop listening. The most effective reminders are simple and brief. If behavior expectations are clear, there's no need to go into a long explanation.

PAY ATTENTION TO THE SMALL THINGS

When the noise just begins to rise above a productive level is the time to ring the bell and remind students to use softer voices. When a group is about to get off task is the time to step in and say, "Remind us what you're supposed to be doing right now." If teachers wait until the noise level has become raucous or until the group has been off task for ten minutes, their words will have less impact.

Redirecting language

Redirecting language is used when a student's behavior has clearly gone off track and needs to be stopped immediately. The teacher calmly and clearly tells the child to stop and explains exactly what the child needs to do instead. Redirecting language is always given as a statement, never a question. The goal is to stop the misbehavior quickly so that the child can regain control and positive behavior can be restored as soon as possible.

Following are some examples of redirecting language:

- Daphne throws the markers across the table instead of handing them to José. The teacher says, "Daphne, in our class we hand markers over. Hand the marker to José now."

- Gavin taps and pokes his neighbors during a meeting. The teacher says, "Gavin, hands in your lap."

- Eric is so eager to offer his own ideas that he often interrupts others in his group before they are finished. The teacher says, "Eric, our rule says to let everyone finish speaking. Slow down and wait until each person is done before giving your thoughts."

- Students are being careless with cleaning up art materials. Paper is getting crumpled, markers are uncapped, work areas are messy. The teacher says, "Our rule says to take good care of our materials. Start this cleanup over."

Here are a few tips for using redirecting language effectively:

BE FIRM WHEN NEEDED

Being firm is not the same as being mean, but it's easy to confuse the two. In an effort to avoid being mean, many teachers shy away from being firm. This does a great disservice to everyone. Students grow uncertain about limits, and teachers lose their authority to establish those limits. Students follow the rules when they feel like it; teachers enforce the rules when it's easy to do so. Generally, this creates an atmosphere of confusion and anxiety.

There are many, many times in the daily life of the classroom when firm is exactly what's called for. A simple guideline to keep in mind is "If you mean no, then say no." No hedging, no beating around the bush. "No, you may not use the materials in that closet" rather than "I'd rather you didn't use the materials in that closet, okay?"

DON'T ASK A QUESTION WHEN YOU MEAN TO BE DIRECTIVE

Instead of asking, "Could you please put your brushes down and look at me?" say, "Put your brushes down and look at me." This is not the same as being harsh, sarcastic, or disrespectful. The tone of voice is direct and firm.

PAY ATTENTION TO TONE AND VOLUME

Consider the many different ways of saying "Come over here and sit down, Danny." The tone could be neutral, loaded with exasperation, or sound more like a plea than a directive. It could be said in a whisper (for only Danny to hear), in a medium volume, or in an all-out scream.

Most children are keenly aware of the subtle and not-so-subtle alterations in meaning caused by tone and volume. While teachers may not always be able to control the negative tone that slyly slips in or the raised volume that makes a directive sound more like a threat, it's important to continue to pay attention to tone and volume and strive to match them to the intended message.

KEEP IT SIMPLE AND CLEAR

Often a single phrase or directive is all that's needed. Instead of "Class, remember how we talked about how hard it is to hear each other when everyone is calling out at once. It's really important that you raise your hand if you have something to say. All of your ideas are important and I want everyone to be heard," try "Meeting rules" or "Raise your hand to speak."

SOMETIMES, USE HUMOR

A teacher might give literally hundreds of reminders and redirections in the course of a normal school day. If you're beginning to feel like a broken record, it might be time to infuse some humor into the situation, as in the following example:

> A teacher has stepped out of the classroom for a few minutes to speak to the principal, leaving the class in the care of an instructional assistant. When the teacher returns, the classroom is noisy and chaotic. He turns off the light, signaling students to stop what they're doing and look at him. He says, "This couldn't possibly be the same class that I left a few minutes ago. I think we need some magic to get the real class back. I'm going to close my eyes for a minute. When I say 'poof' I want the classroom to magically change back to how it was when I left."

The process of changing language

Often teachers who want to change their language go through a conscious process. Here are some strategies that can help:

- Listen consciously to your words.

- Tape-record or videotape yourself in the classroom for a short period of time. Listen to the tape to detect your language patterns.

- Have a colleague observe you for fifteen minutes, recording the words and phrases you use most frequently.

- Focus on changing one phrase at a time.

- Agree with some colleagues to focus on changing the same words or phrases at the same time.

- Enlist students to help you change your language habits. Second/third grade teacher Gail Zimmerman asked students to use phrases such as "I notice . . ."; "Show me . . ."; and "Remind us . . ." with each other and to remind her when she needed to use them. Asking students to help is a way to model being a learner who makes mistakes and works to fix them.

- When you do make a mistake, try fixing it in the moment. You might say something like "Let's erase that. What I wanted to say was . . ."

- Pause before speaking to give yourself a chance to think.

- Post a list of desirable words and phrases in your classroom for easy reference. Or write them on a card that you can easily carry around and refer to.

- Rely more on nonverbal signals and cues as a way to get students' attention. This will reduce the amount of "teacher talk," allowing you to focus more fully on the most important language patterns.

Through all of this, remember that change takes time. Be patient with yourself and celebrate the incremental improvements you make along the way. (For more information about teacher language, please see *The Power of Our Words* by Paula Denton, EdD.)

Review: Bringing the Rules to Life

1. Use structured discussion to help children think through how to apply the rules to everyday situations.

2. Use interactive modeling to refresh children's understanding of classroom routines.

3. Use role-playing to help children make good choices in potentially tricky situations.

4. Use teacher language to reinforce children's positive actions and to help them prepare for upcoming situations.

WORKS CITED

Belluck, Pam. (2000, October 18). New Advice for Parents: Saying 'That's Great!' May Not Be. *New York Times*, A14.

Bronson, Po, and Merryman, Ashley. (2009). *Nurture Shock: New Thinking About Children.* New York: Twelve.

Denton, Paula, EdD. (2007). *The Power of Our Words: Teacher Language That Helps Children Learn.* Turners Falls, MA: Northeast Foundation for Children, Inc.

Dreikurs, Rudolf (with Soltz, Vicki). (1964). *Children: The Challenge.* New York: Plume.

Nelsen, Jane. (1996). *Positive Discipline.* (Rev. ed.) New York: Ballantine.

Wood, Chip. (Speaker). (1998). *Seven Principles of the Responsive Classroom: A Keynote Address.* Greenfield, MA: Northeast Foundation for Children, Inc.

Responding to Misbehavior

Purposes and Reflections

If we've taken the proactive steps of teaching children the social and academic skills they need in order to learn effectively, providing structures that create a safe learning environment, making sure our expectations are developmentally appropriate, and checking that our teaching is relevant and accessible to all students, we've done a lot of the work of discipline. But there will still be times when we need to respond to children's misbehavior. The proactive work we've done can make our responses more effective and reduce the amount of time spent responding to misbehavior but it won't completely eliminate children's misbehavior.

It's not hard to understand why children misbehave. Just think about all the reasons you might have for breaking a rule. For example, when you're going fifty in a forty-mile-per-hour zone, you might be doing it because:

- You're late for a meeting.

- You didn't know it was a forty-mile-per-hour zone.

- You don't think it should be a forty-mile-per-hour zone.

- You don't think you'll get caught.

- You like how it feels to go fast.

- You didn't know you were going that fast.

- You're frustrated that your last meeting went so late and it's "their" fault you have to go so fast now.

- Everyone else is going fifty.

Like all of us, children will have many moments when impulse wins over reason, desire over logic, feelings over rational thought. They will get curious, they will get carried away, they will forget. As every adult knows, it can take a lifetime to learn how to control our impulses and regulate our behavior.

Also keep in mind that children are still in the early stages of learning the rules of the world, no less the rules of the school. They're constantly trying to figure out what the larger world expects of them, and they do much of this learning by doing. Through their exploring and experimenting, they come to understand what's acceptable and what isn't during a meeting, on the playground, at the grocery store, during sports practice, at a play, on the bus.

Experimenting with rules and testing limits is a normal part of children's development. It's how they construct their understanding of social expectations. As we all know, some children are much more persistent in their testing than others, but almost every child has some need to experiment with behavior.

Child psychologist Robert MacKenzie describes children's misbehavior as research, testing the limits in order to find out how the adults in their lives will respond. With their misbehavior, these researchers are asking "What's OK? What's not OK? Who's in control? How far can I go? And what happens when I go too far?" (MacKenzie, 1997, pp. 32–34)

In the process of doing this testing and experimenting, students will make lots of mistakes. Just as with learning an academic subject such as math or reading or science, students need repeated practice to solidify their learning around positive behavior expectations. We can use students' mistakes as opportunities to teach self-control and responsibility.

To do this, we need to hold on to our empathy. Having empathy doesn't mean we let go of accountability; instead, we hold children accountable, but with empathy for why they might be misbehaving and faith that they can choose a better way to behave. In the process, we might just help them learn to manage their own behavior.

Goals in responding to children's misbehavior

One important goal in responding to misbehavior is to stop the negative behavior and re-establish positive behavior as quickly and simply as possible so that we can return the child to learning and we can continue teaching. Doing this is essential to maintaining a safe and orderly classroom.

We also want to give children opportunities to learn from their mistakes. It is through making mistakes; experiencing relevant, nonpunitive consequences; and, when appropriate, processing the mistakes with a caring adult that students eventually internalize the rules.

Rather than simply telling children what to do, we want them to develop their own understanding of why it's not safe to run in the halls, why it's distracting to a speaker when classmates are poking one another, and why it's hurtful to laugh at someone's mistakes. In this way, they will gain a deeper understanding of the rules and learn to take responsibility for their actions.

The goals in responding to misbehavior, then, are to:

- Maintain a safe and orderly classroom

- Help students recognize and fix their mistakes

- Help students develop internal control of their behavior

It's in the spirit of maintaining a safe learning environment, preserving children's dignity, and helping them learn from their mistakes, rather than punishing them or making them pay for their mistakes, that the following strategies for responding to misbehavior are offered.

Getting Started

Begin with an assumption of good intentions

An important foundation for responding effectively to children's misbehavior is to begin with the assumption of children's good intentions. There are so many things we don't know about the children and situations that arise in the classroom. For example, when we see Angel ripping up Tony's writing assignment, we don't know what Tony wrote about Angel on that paper. When we see Yazhe jab Ariela, we don't know what Ariela might have done to provoke it. And when Sonya pounds her desk in frustration during writing time, we have no idea what might have happened to prompt such anger before she came to school that morning.

Rather than making quick, negative judgments—Angel is up to his antics again, Yazhe is so aggressive, Sonya is always trying to avoid work—we would do better to learn more. We might begin with a simple request for facts: "What's going on here?" Or we can make an observation followed by a question: "Looks like you need some help. Do you want to talk about it now or take a few minutes to cool off?"

One question that's probably not very helpful to ask children in the moment is why: "Why did you tear up his paper?" "Why did you jab Ariela?" "Why are you pounding your desk?" In the heat of the moment, this question, even if well-intentioned, will sound accusatory to children and make them defensive. Often, the children's response will be to quickly blame the other person or to say blankly, "I don't know." And in many cases, they honestly don't.

Stop the misbehavior

The number one priority of responding to misbehavior is to stop the misbehavior and restore positive behavior as quickly as possible. This sounds obvious, but so often teachers skip this step. Children need to hear the words "Stop now" to break the momentum of their running, yelling, teasing, etc., and change course. To do this, teachers need to observe children carefully in order to see and consistently respond to small misbehaviors before they become more entrenched patterns. Simple cues, teacher language, and teacher proximity are all useful tools to use in these instances.

Use visual and verbal cues

Marianne rolls her eyes at a friend while another student is sharing. Kenya starts to fiddle with the puzzles on the shelf behind her during a lesson. A small group gets off task. Pauline whispers to her neighbor instead of doing her math work. Yaser cuts in line. There are many times in the life of the classroom when a visual or verbal cue is all that's needed to stop the misbehavior and help students get back on track.

The cue can be as simple as saying the child's name or looking into the child's eyes. Essentially the cue communicates, "I know that you can do better than that. Now let's see you do it."

Here are some common and effective visual and verbal cues:

- Make brief eye contact with the child.

- Say the child's name.

- Use reminding and redirecting language, such as "Quiet feet, Sean" or "What do our rules say about sharing materials?" (See Chapter Two for more information on reminding and redirecting language.)

- Nod at the child.

- Give a hand signal such as a writing gesture, a finger against the lips, etc.

Notice that none of these cues requires the teacher to stop what she's doing or to explain the rule or expectation. They also minimize calling attention to the child. The communication is between the teacher and student involved. The teacher assumes that the student knows what to do but just needs a little nudge to do it.

These simple cues are most effective when they're given before the misbehavior has gone on for too long. Obviously if a child doesn't immediately respond to a visual or verbal cue, then it's time to be more directive. However, giving children this opportunity to recognize their mistakes and correct themselves in the moment helps them to preserve their dignity and develop self-control.

When using visual cues and gestures, it's important to pay attention to body language. If a teacher is feeling angry or frustrated, simple eye contact might carry a strongly punitive message. Remember the old chant from elementary school years, "No more pencils, no more books, no more teachers' dirty looks"? There is often a fine line between the reminding or redirecting look and the "dirty" look.

Increased teacher proximity

Sometimes all that's needed to re-establish positive behavior is for the teacher to move next to a child. For example, if second grader Maria is kicking the rungs of her chair during a classmate's presentation, her teacher might simply stand next to her, which can be a cue to Maria to have quiet feet. The teacher would continue to stand there for a few minutes to ensure that Maria's feet do indeed stay still.

Don't overuse cues and reminders

All this said, keep in mind that cues and reminders can have a damaging effect if they're overused. In classrooms where teachers always give a certain number of reminders before taking further action, students quickly figure out that they don't really have to control themselves until the second or third or fourth time around. They become more focused on keeping track of the reminders than keeping track of their behavior.

Use logical consequences if needed

Logical consequences are also an effective way to stop misbehavior. In addition to stopping the misbehavior, logical consequences can help children see the connection between their behavior and the effect it has on others. They help children understand that we are all responsible for the consequences of our actions.

The three Rs of logical consequences

Teachers sometimes confuse logical consequences with punishment. However, the two approaches to discipline differ in both intent and application. Unlike punishment, logical consequences are relevant, realistic, and respectful.

RELEVANT

The consequence is directly related to the child's action. For example, if a group of children ask to work together on a project and then use the time to talk about their weekend plans, a relevant consequence would be that they lose the opportunity to work together that day.

REALISTIC

The consequence must be something that is realistic for the child to do and the teacher to follow through on. For example, a logical consequence for a child who writes on a desk is for that child to clean the desk. However, holding the child back from lunch or a special area class in order to clean the desk would not be reasonable and could feel punitive. Instead, the teacher could ask the child to identify a time to clean the desk that day or the teacher could find a time that does not take the child away from other important tasks.

RESPECTFUL

A logical consequence is communicated with respect for the child. The teacher is firm but caring and focuses on the specific behavior rather than making general judgments about the child's character. For example, when issuing a logical consequence to a student who has pushed a classmate, the teacher might say, "Stop. Hands off. Our rules say to treat each other with respect" rather than "Stop being such a bully."

These three Rs go a long way towards keeping responses to misbehavior nonpunitive. But there is no question that even with the most thoughtful use of logical consequences, children will sometimes protest or resist. They may deny any wrongdoing or complain that "you're always picking on me." It can be a painful and difficult process for children to recognize and take responsibility for their mistakes, as it can be for adults.

It's important for teachers to remember that they can't control how children feel. Often children feel bad simply for having made a mistake, for having lost their self-control or attracted negative attention. Their protests may be as much a sign of these feelings about themselves as their feelings about the teacher's response. As teachers, our job is to help them restore the situation without further humiliation.

Punishment versus logical consequences: An example

Six-year-old Jacob is zooming around the classroom when suddenly he trips and falls into Michelle's block building. Michelle lets out a scream and the teacher comes over.

PUNISHMENT

A teacher using a punishment approach to discipline might say loudly to Jacob in front of the other children, "I've told you over and over not to run in this classroom. Now see what you've done with your carelessness." Feeling irritated, the teacher might continue, "Go sit in that chair and don't move until it's time for lunch."

LOGICAL CONSEQUENCES

A teacher who uses logical consequences might also feel irritated but would take a deep breath and begin by thinking calmly about what just happened: "Michelle is upset because Jacob knocked over her building. I need to talk with Jacob."

Taking Jacob aside, the teacher says, "When kids run in the classroom, accidents often happen. That's why our rule says to be safe. What do you think you could do to help?"

"I don't know."

"Maybe you could help stack up the blocks so Michelle can build again."

Jacob nods and the teacher walks back with him to the block area. Michelle lets Jacob help gather and stack the scattered blocks. She declines his offer to help rebuild her structure.

Here are some key differences between the two approaches:

	Punishment	Logical Consequences
Intention	To ensure compliance by using external controls that make the child feel ashamed or bad in other ways	To help children recognize the effects of their actions and develop internal controls
Underlying belief	Children will do better only because they fear punishment and will seek to avoid it	Children want to do better and can do better with reflection and practice
Teacher's approach and tone	Reacts automatically with little thought; voice is angry and punitive	Gathers more information before reacting; voice is calm and matter-of-fact
Nature of the consequence	Not related to the behavior or the damage done; not reasonable for the child to do	Related to the behavior; reasonable for the child to do
Message to the child	The child is the problem	The damage done, not the child, is the problem

Three types of logical consequences

There are three basic types of logical consequences: "You break it, you fix it," loss of privilege, and time-out. While there are significant variations in what each looks like at different grade levels, generally all logical consequences fall within one of these categories.

"YOU BREAK IT, YOU FIX IT"

This is as simple and clear as it sounds. If children break something or make a mess, whether intentionally or not, the teacher helps them take responsibility for fixing it or cleaning it up. If you jiggle the table and make someone mess up her work, you help her do it over again. If you knock someone down on the playing field, you help him up, ask if he's okay, and go with him to the first aid office if needed.

LOSS OF PRIVILEGE

When a child abuses a privilege such as using classroom materials safely or taking on a classroom responsibility, a logical consequence would be to take away that privilege temporarily, perhaps for a class period or a day.

For example, if a student with the job of line leader has a hard time walking quietly and safely in line, she may lose her line leader responsibility for the day. Or if a student consistently uses the watercolor brush in a way that damages the bristles, he might not be able to choose watercolors as an option during choice time until he's had a chance to practice correct use of the brush and has demonstrated his understanding to the teacher.

The purpose of removing a privilege is not to punish the child, but to protect the child and the group and to preserve the integrity of the rules. Once the child demonstrates readiness to handle the responsibility, it's important to give the privilege back. The goal is for children to show that they can be responsible, not to suffer for being irresponsible. Through words and actions, a teacher demonstrates faith in children's ability to learn responsibility.

TIME-OUT

This is a strategy used to help children learn self-control. A child who is disrupting the work of the group is asked to leave for a minute or two. During this time, the child is expected to regain self-control so he can come back to the group and participate in a positive way. In some cases, children can decide themselves to go to the time-out spot because they are losing control and need to leave the scene for a while to regain composure.

In the following chapters, two teachers show in detail how one might introduce and use time-out in different grades. However, because time-out is so often misunderstood, here are some immediate guidelines for using this strategy:

Explain the purpose. Because children may have experienced punitive uses of time-out, it's important that teachers explain clearly that the purpose of time-out in this classroom is to give children a chance to calm down and regain self-control. It's important to let students know that after they calm down, they will be welcomed back into the group. Letting children know that sometimes they might decide for themselves when they need a time-out can also help remove the stigma surrounding it.

Consider what to call it. Many teachers feel that the term "time-out" carries such negative connotations that they prefer to use a term such as "take a break" or "rest stop." Children, especially in the older grades, may enjoy helping to come up with an appropriate term to use.

Choose a good spot. There should be one or two designated time-out places in the room—perhaps a chair, a cushion, or a beanbag. The spot should be neither isolated nor in the thick of activity. This gives children the separation they need in order to calm down, yet allows them to keep track of what's going on in the classroom so that they can join in the work when they come back. To keep the child safe, the teacher needs to be able to see the time-out area from anywhere in the room.

As students move into middle school, they may no longer require a designated place for time-out. Able to understand that the idea is to cool down, they generally can choose an appropriate place to go for this purpose and appreciate being given this flexibility.

Explicitly teach time-out procedures. This means talking about, modeling, and practicing how to do time-out. Older students will need less practice but will like sharing ideas for pulling themselves together, such as looking at a poster, taking deep breaths, writing in a journal, and squeezing a stress ball.

For children of all ages, be sure this teaching covers the following:

- Going to the time-out spot quickly, quietly, calmly, and promptly

- Doing whatever it takes to regain self-control as long as it's quiet and doesn't distract the class

- Coming back from time-out quietly and rejoining the work of the group

Remember also to teach the rest of the class what to do when a classmate needs to go to time-out. Talk about, model, and let children practice leaving the classmate alone, going on with the classroom activity as usual, and welcoming the classmate back when she returns.

Clarify who decides when the child should return. The ultimate goal is for children to be able to tell when they're in control and ready to return. But to reach that goal, teachers might need to explicitly teach children how to calm down and how to know they're back in control. And in some classes, the teacher might decide that the majority of children aren't ready for the responsibility of knowing when to return from time-out and will retain the decision-making.

Even when the teacher feels children are ready to come back on their own, there might be times when a child comes back from time-out before having regained control or lingers longer than necessary. In this case, the teacher should take over the decision for that child the next time.

Use time-out just as a child is beginning to lose control. Don't wait until the behavior has escalated and the child has lost face with peers. Using time-out early helps preserve children's relationships and the teacher's feelings of empathy toward students. It can be tough, for example, to feel empathy when a child has become aggressive.

If a child has progressed to being fully out of control, teachers need another strategy, perhaps one that involves the principal, a guidance counselor, or other support staff.

Always use a calm, quiet voice to tell a child to go to time-out. Even better, also establish a visual signal to give this direction when possible. This avoids drawing attention to the child.

Never enter into a negotiation in the moment. An important purpose of time-out is to allow the work of the group to go on when a student is misbehaving. Discussing the situation with the student will only disrupt the group further. Moreover, the student is usually not in a frame of mind at the moment to discuss the situation reasonably. However, in introducing time-out, it's important for teachers to assure students that they can always talk with the teacher about the situation later.

Use time-out democratically. At one point or another, almost all children in a classroom lose their cool and can use a method to collect themselves. It's important that students see that time-out is used for anyone who needs it and not just the same two or three children.

Have a system for time-out in another room. Many teachers set up a "buddy teacher" system for times when a student refuses to go to time-out, continues to be disruptive in time-out, or continues to be disruptive after a time-out. In those cases, the teacher has the child take a time-out in the buddy teacher's room. This prevents the situation from escalating into a power struggle and allows the teacher to go on teaching the class. (See box on pages 84 and 85 for more information on buddy teacher time-out.)

Buddy Teacher Time-Out

When a child needs a longer break or needs to leave the classroom in order to calm down, the teacher can call on the assistance of a buddy teacher who will take the child to a different classroom for a period of time. This can prevent the situation from escalating into a power struggle and allows the teacher to go on teaching the class. Here's what it might look like:

> *Seven-year-old Valerie has difficulty controlling her emotional outbursts. She and Ms. Morgan have been working on this all year and she's improved greatly and can often get herself back in control by sitting in the break chair. But today, when Ms. Morgan sends Valerie to take-a-break after Valerie interrupts another student, Valerie sits in the chair muttering under her breath and loudly kicking the rungs. Ms. Morgan calmly asks Jason to go get the buddy teacher, Mrs. Johnston, and then continues with the math lesson. When Mrs. Johnston arrives, Ms. Morgan directs her towards Valerie. Mrs. Johnston goes to Valerie and says quietly, "Come with me." Valerie is familiar with this routine and leaves with Mrs. Johnston.*

Early in the year, it's important for teachers to identify their buddy teacher(s) and plan together how to use this strategy. In the moment of needing to call on the buddy teacher, here are some basic steps to follow:

1. *Direct another student or an adult in the classroom to tell the buddy teacher she is needed.*

2. *Continue teaching the class while the messenger goes to the buddy teacher and gives the message.*

3. *Buddy teacher and messenger return to your classroom and the messenger returns to work.*

4. *The child who is having difficulty goes with the buddy teacher back to the buddy teacher's room. There is no conversation or problem-solving. The child sits quietly in the buddy teacher's room.*

5. *When ready, the classroom teacher brings the child back and the child joins the ongoing work of the classroom.*

As with time-out, it's important to explain to the children the purpose of buddy teacher time-out and to teach procedures for going, staying, and returning. It's also important to discuss and model the response of other children in the class when a classmate goes with a buddy teacher and, even more important, when the classmate returns. Losing control and going with the buddy teacher might be embarrassing but teachers can minimize that embarrassment by modeling the procedure and discussing appropriate reactions.

Remember that time-out does not work for all children. If a teacher sends a child over and over to time-out without seeing any improvement in behavior, or if a child crumbles or becomes extremely distraught at even one use of time-out, more than likely the child needs a different strategy. Seek help from colleagues, parents, and counselors, and consider other problem-solving strategies. (See Appendix A for a summary of problem-solving strategies.)

Introducing logical consequences to students

Why is it sometimes hard to follow the rules?

What are the hardest rules to follow? What makes them hard to follow?

What are the easiest rules to follow?

What's an example of a time you didn't follow the rules?

How do you feel when you're not following the rules?

How do you feel when you are following the rules?

These are some of the questions a teacher might ask students in opening a conversation about logical consequences. In these conversations, it's important to convey the following messages:

- We are all working together on learning to follow the rules.

- Following the rules takes lots of practice.

- Everyone makes mistakes. We all forget or choose not to follow rules from time to time.

- When you forget or choose not to follow a rule, it's my job to help you get back on track and help you learn to do better next time.

Carefully define the term "logical consequence" if you use it

In introducing the concept of logical consequences to students, not all teachers use the term "logical consequences." If teachers do use the term, it's important that they define it as a way to solve problems, get back on track, and learn. This helps take away the punitive ring that the term may have.

For example, a teacher might begin by saying, "We're all working on following our rules. Let's think for a minute about what happens when we follow our rules." The teacher might give some specific examples of rule following (such as letting everyone join an activity, working hard with partners even if they're not your best friends, and cleaning the paint brushes carefully after using them) and then talk with children about the positive consequences of these actions.

Next, the teacher might say, "We'll all make mistakes from time to time. Sometimes we might forget a rule, sometimes we might choose not to follow one. What happens when we don't follow a rule—for example, the rules we just talked about?" The teacher now guides children in thinking about the possible problems that might result, including safety risks, hurt feelings, work left undone, and others' inability to do their work.

"In our classroom," the teacher might continue, "when students don't follow a rule, it'll be my job to help them get back on track, fix any problems they created, and learn to follow the rule next time. One way I'll be doing that is by using something called logical consequences." In this way, the teacher casts "logical consequences" in an objective light, removing the connotation of shame and punishment that children may associate with that term.

Give examples of logical consequences

Whether or not teachers use the term "logical consequences" with students, what's important is that they give examples of logical consequences. A teacher might say, for instance, "A student is running in the classroom and accidentally knocks over another student's diorama. If that happens, I might tell that child to help repair the damage to the diorama."

Or the teacher might say, "If we're using the staplers for an art project and someone is using a stapler in an unsafe way, a logical consequence would be for that person to stop using the stapler for the rest of the day. The person could try again the next day, maybe with the teacher watching to help them use it safely."

By giving several such examples, the teacher lets students know ahead of time what sorts of things will happen when they break the rules. Children will feel more comfortable and assured when they have this specific information. They'll know that their teacher expects them to live by the rules, and that if they don't, the teacher will help them to stay safe physically and emotionally and learn to do better next time. Without these examples from teachers, many students will feel anxious and uncertain. Some will constantly test the boundaries in search of clarity. Others will withdraw in fear.

The teacher decides on logical consequences

Choosing a logical consequence is not a collaborative process. When introducing logical consequences, a teacher may ask children to come up with some appropriate consequences for various hypothetical situations. Such a discussion can help children understand the intention and characteristics of this way of handling rule breaking. In real rule-breaking situations, however, the teacher is in charge of deciding on the consequence.

Choosing an appropriate logical consequence is a complex decision requiring knowledge and mature judgment. Most elementary and middle

school students have a tremendously difficult time distinguishing between logical consequences and punishments. Asked to decide on a logical consequence, students are likely to dole out harsh punishments and judgments. Deciding on logical consequences for other students is not a position elementary and middle grade students should ever be in.

When Is Taking Away Recess a Logical Consequence?

Children need outdoor play much like they need food and sleep. That's why teachers should only take away short periods of recess, if at all.

Taking away recess is a logical consequence only when:

- The misbehavior took place during recess or immediately preceding recess (for example, not getting ready for recess when asked to)

- It's realistic for the teacher to supervise the child (for example, does not require the teacher to give up prep time or miss a team meeting to stay in the classroom with the child)

Taking away recess is not a logical consequence when:

- It's used repeatedly

- It's used for behavior not connected to recess

- It creates a situation that will make it more difficult for the child to succeed

- It creates a hardship for the teacher

The challenge of choosing a logical consequence: One size does not fit all

Each child—and situation—is unique. There is no such thing as one size fits all when it comes to responding to misbehavior. Different situations call for different responses. When children misbehave, they give us valuable information about what they need.

In *Maintaining Sanity in the Classroom* Dreikurs, Pepper, and Grunwald write about the need that all people have for a sense of belonging and a sense of importance, or significance. (1982) Researcher Edward Deci frames these fundamental human needs as the need for autonomy (the freedom to control oneself), relatedness (being connected to others), and competence (the ability to achieve desired outcomes). (Deci, 1995) Both Dreikurs et al. and Deci remind us that when people's basic psychological needs are not met, they often act out in negative ways. Understanding what's behind a child's misbehavior can help a teacher to choose an effective response.

Here are a few questions a teacher might ask when a child misbehaves:

- Are expectations clear? Too high? Too low?

- Is this behavior part of a pattern? Or is it an isolated situation?

- Is the child testing the limits? Is the child engaging in a power struggle?

- What's been helpful for this child in the past? What hasn't been helpful?

At the same time, the teacher needs to respond quickly to stop the misbehavior. Here are two general guidelines that will help teachers quickly choose an effective response:

If it doesn't seem obvious, it's probably not logical

The key is to look at each situation and ask, "What's the problem here? Hurt feelings? A safety issue? Distraction from work? Disturbing others? How can I stop the problematic action? And given what I know about this child and these circumstances, how can I help this child see and fix the problem?"

If the consequence doesn't become obvious after this reflection, then it's quite likely that the situation requires something other than a logical consequence. It's also possible that in that particular situation, no imposed consequence is needed. If a child forgets to get a permission form signed and therefore cannot participate in a field trip or a photo-taking session, not being able to take part is itself a significant enough consequence that it no doubt teaches the child a great deal about taking responsibility. In that case, there's no need for the teacher to impose a further consequence.

Sometimes two steps are needed

There are times when we get so angry and frustrated that we can't think clearly. In times like these, when emotions obscure logic, the best thing is to do what is needed to respectfully stop the misbehavior in the moment (for example, removing the child from the situation). Later, after everyone has had time to cool off, you can decide if any further action is needed.

You might set up a time to talk with the child after lunch, after recess, or at some later point in the day. Keep in mind, however, that this waiting time can be a great source of anxiety for some children. If this might be the case for a particular child, keep the cool-off period as short as possible.

Many teachers recognize that during these times of anger and frustration, they themselves need a time-out. They may call on an assistant or a colleague to be with their class for a few minutes while they take a walk down the hall. If this isn't possible, they might change the class activity so that students are working independently. The teacher can then sit quietly at her desk for a few minutes.

Additional Tips for the Use of Logical Consequences

The following tips, compiled by primary teacher Deborah Porter, come from various teachers who have used the approach to discipline described in this book. In Chapter Four, Deborah expands on these tips, showing how they've played out in her K–2 classroom.

Know the child

The same rule-breaking behavior may demand very different logical consequences with different children, since what's motivating each child and what each child understands determine what that child needs to learn and what problem needs to be fixed. The point is never to apply consequences uniformly, but to understand where each child is coming from and choose a consequence that makes sense for that child.

Have preset consequences for certain situations

The "know the child" tip notwithstanding, there are times—particularly when safety is a concern—when a preset response is justified. For example, a teacher might decide that any child who runs in the halls would, for a period of time, have to be accompanied when leaving the classroom. Each teacher should decide what situations require such nonnegotiable, preset consequences.

Avoid lecturing

When using a logical consequence, the less said the better. Let the consequence do the job. If the consequence is well chosen, it will be more powerful than any teacher words. Additional explanations can easily undermine that power and add to any classroom disruption that the child's behavior may have caused.

Rely on colleagues for help

Beyond setting up a buddy teacher system (see box on pages 84–85 for information about buddy teacher time-out), there are informal ways for teachers to get crucial support from each other. If the same behavior problem keeps showing up in your classroom or if a particular child makes you especially angry or frustrated, talk with colleagues about it. Often, good solutions emerge from the collective experience and wisdom of teachers and staff.

Have a re-entry check-in or conversation if a child must leave the room

If the logical consequence involves the child leaving the room—to go to a buddy teacher's room or to the principal's office, for example—it's crucial that the teacher have a conversation with the child before bringing the child back into the classroom. The conversation will be about what happened, what needs to be done now, and how to prevent similar situations in the future. Taking the time to do this step shows the child that she or he is still liked and respected, that relationships are intact. And it reassures the teacher that the child is ready to come back to the class.

Try, try again

Responding to misbehavior is challenging, perhaps one of the most challenging aspects of teaching. Even the most experienced teachers make mistakes. But the most experienced teachers will also be the first to say that teachers must allow themselves to make mistakes, just as they allow students to make them. And just as we tell our students—without shaming them—to "try, try again," we must allow ourselves to try again without self-defeating judgments, but with the spirit of learning to do it better next time. As Dreikurs et al. (1982) point out, it's not the mistake, but what one does about it, that's important. In time, mistakes will give way to successes.

Review: Responding to Misbehavior

1. The first priority is to stop the misbehavior as quickly and simply as possible so that the teacher can continue teaching and the children can continue learning.

2. Often, simple cues such as a gesture or increased teacher proximity are all that is needed to stop the misbehavior and restore order.

3. Use of logical consequences is also an effective strategy for responding to misbehavior.

4. There are three kinds of logical consequences: "you break it, you fix it," loss of privilege, and time-out.

5. Logical consequences are relevant, realistic, and respectful.

6. Use structured discussion to introduce the concept of logical consequences.

7. The responsibility for deciding on and issuing logical consequences resides with the teacher.

WORKS CITED

Deci, Edward L. (with Flaste, Richard). (1995). *Why We Do What We Do.* New York: Penguin.

Dreikurs, Rudolf, Pepper, Floy C., and Grunwald, Bernice Bronia. (1982). *Maintaining Sanity in the Classroom: Classroom Management Techniques.* (2nd ed.). New York: Harper and Row.

MacKenzie, Robert J. (1997, fall). Setting Limits in the Classroom. *American Educator.*

CHAPTER FOUR | By Deborah Porter

Grades K–2

I was at the bakery counter in the supermarket one day, when a little girl came skipping up waving a dollar bill.

"My Grandma gave me a dollar to buy donut holes," she proclaimed to the clerk. "How many holes can I get for a dollar?"

The woman behind the counter told her that she could get six.

"Six! That's a lot," the girl replied. Then, without missing a beat, she said, "If I had two dollars I could get twelve of them!"

"Yep," the store clerk replied. "Donut holes are six for sixty-nine cents."

"Oh, but I only have a dollar," the girl said, looking slightly confused.

The clerk explained that sixty-nine cents was less than a dollar and that she would get six holes and some change back.

In her excitement, the girl danced to her grandmother to tell her the good news. Then she danced back to place her order, keeping careful count as she picked out the kind of donut holes she wanted. Then once again to the grandmother to report what she had decided on, and back one last time to pay her dollar.

When the girl finally got both her change and the donut holes, she could hardly contain her excitement. As she departed she exclaimed with great enthusiasm, "You don't need to worry about me returning these donuts. I'm going to love them!"

The Dance of Learning

As I watched this little girl's dance of excitement, I thought about how closely it matched what might have been going on in her mind as she moved back and forth between knowing and confusion, between the joy of making her way in the world and bafflement at how something would actually work out.

Every day in the classroom, I feel as if the children and I do this little dance: I, as I try to understand each child and what that child most needs; and the children, as they learn new concepts, fitting them together with what they already know about the world. The trick of the dance is to hop back and forth between confusion and knowing with light, quick steps so that we are neither flying too fast, trying to absorb too much—nor stuck in place, refusing to evolve in the face of new information.

Doing this dance of learning requires us to take risks, to be willing to give things a try even though we know there is the possibility of failure. When I think of classroom practices around behavior and discipline, I think always of supporting children's risk taking. Creating a positive classroom environment allows children to feel safe about taking risks, and when children feel safe about taking risks, the very quality of their learning goes up.

But how can we find time for a social curriculum, when we're already straining to cover all the academics? I believe it's never a matter of choosing between the academic and the social curriculum. Rather, it's a matter of addressing the social so that we can address the academic, and addressing the academic so that we can address the social.

Children need to know how to take turns, listen, choose respectful words, and use appropriate body language when working together on math problems or doing a group science experiment. They need to know how to read, add and subtract, make charts, and use other academic skills to decide who gets to take the lunch counts this week or how four people can share the paints fairly. If we don't take the time to teach the social curriculum, the academic curriculum is diminished.

Just as it's impossible to separate the social from the academic, it is not easy to speak of rules without considering all the elements of the entire classroom. A commitment to establishing positive behavior expectations and supporting children's efforts at positive behavior is embedded in everything that gives rise to a safe and productive learning community: friendship, collaboration, meaningful work, growth and learning, mental well-being, and physical health and safety. And so, as part of creating a classroom where every child can learn, we establish rules and explicitly teach children how to follow those rules.

In an even larger sense, we are also teaching for the time when we will not be there. The authority of our position rests on this reach beyond the time when students are in our classrooms and our schools. We must therefore use techniques that give children the power to think and act ethically for themselves. Just as we teach children to read so that they might be able to participate in a literate world, so too, we must teach children to care for themselves and others so that they might later participate in a democratic society.

Before School Starts

August: My goals begin to take shape

The rule-creation process described in this book begins with children articulating their learning goals for the year. Like the children, I, too, begin my year by formulating my goals. Along about mid-August, I start to put my classroom in order, hoping to find the perfect way to arrange it. Each year the physical task of arranging the room helps me refocus on the day-to-day life of the classroom, on the children, and on the work we do together. This is when I at last let go of the year before, whether it feels finished or not, and begin to get excited about the year ahead.

As I put the final touches on the room, I dream of what the year might look like. I see children working in all the areas of the room, writing stories, painting pictures, and building grand structures or complicated machines. I see them reading books, playing games, and solving problems together. The room is filled with a busy hum, with friendly exchanges and earnest collaboration. This is when my own goals begin to take shape.

My biggest hope: "I would like us to do fewer things but do them well."

In my more than thirty years of teaching, I have seen so many changes, both in my own teaching and in the realm of public education itself. I've lived through various educational movements, each with its pluses and minuses, each requiring accommodation and training, each adding to the complexity of our educational institutions.

Amid all the demands that society places on teachers' work, beginning each year with a most important goal has become a key way for me to maintain my own clarity and conviction about my work. One year, my most important goal was to be able to include a child with a severe disability as a full, integral member of the classroom. Another year it was to work more with other teachers. Yet another year it was to focus on literacy routines that would give children the skills they needed while helping them develop their own interests and ideas. This year, my biggest hope is that the children and I will do fewer projects but do them well.

I teach in a building that is beautifully designed. One of its special features is that it feels bigger on the inside than it looks from the outside. I would like our work to be like our building, making us bigger on the inside. I want to avoid filling the day with just the demands and details of someone else's agenda. I want to have our own sacred class time where children have the leisure to explore, share, discuss, and work together.

I know from experience that this will require me to organize and integrate the curriculum in a way that weaves the much needed skill work into interesting and engaging content areas. I'll plan on carving out one hour each day that the children and I can count on as "our" work time. As schedules are made, I will keep this time clear so that it is possible for us to do in-depth projects.

As the children begin to express their own goals, which we will call "hopes and dreams," I will be excited to let them know that I, too, have a most important goal for the year: that the class will be able to do projects together. And as we begin to create the rules, not only will I already have a vision in my mind of what I'll have to do to allow for these projects, but we as a class will think together about what all of us will need to do to allow for them.

The first family conference: Families share their goals for the year

Once the room is set up and before school starts, it is time to invite the children and their parents in for a tour. Each family comes for a thirty- to forty-minute visit. These visits are also an opportunity for me to find out parents' goals and hopes for their children in the coming year. Before the visits, I send out a query to help parents clarify their thinking, and they bring the completed sheet with them to the visit. (See sample query below.) If parents find filling out the written form intimidating or simply

PARENT QUERY: First Planning Conference

Name of parent(s): _____

Name of student: _____

Please answer the following questions to help us plan your child's program:

1. What is your most important hope for your child in school this year?

2. In what ways or areas would you like to see your child grow socially or emotionally?

3. In what ways or areas would you like to see your child grow academically?

haven't had a chance to fill it out, we do it together during the visit. The information on the sheet helps to focus our conversation on what is most important to parents.

In the early grades, parent goals are often the simple, age-old ones: for kindergartners, to enjoy school and make friends; for first graders, to learn to read; and for second graders, to use their skills to learn about a broader world.

Often parents come with their hopes *and* fears, and leave after the conversation with their fears calmed and the sense of possibility that each new school year brings. Of course it is not always that easy to melt away parent concerns, and so I see these conferences as just a beginning, a way to create an important common ground for our shared work ahead.

Helping families share their expertise

When I invite families into a conversation about the coming year, I also ask for their input as the experts on their children. I ask about the child's special interests, friendships, strengths, how the child tends to handle difficult challenges, and the like.

From the very beginning of the year on, I want to hear from parents what they know about their children so that I can better teach the children. Over the years I have found that though I don't always see the children in the same way as the parents do or always agree with the parents' priorities, this first conference is an important beginning to our working together in a constructive way.

The First Days of School

I always seem to wake up with a start on the first day of school. It's no wonder. This business of formulating goals helps to clarify what I and children's families most want, but it is, after all, only the beginning and there is much hard work still to be done. All the routines and rules have yet to be established. I know that simply having all the children come and sit in a circle can be a challenge.

Establishing routines

It takes a few weeks for young children to understand and adjust to school life, even if they've been in school before. There's so much they need to learn. There are lunch routines, work routines, fire drills, playground routines, meeting routines, bathroom routines. During the early weeks of school, all of these need to be carefully taught and practiced.

I introduce many of the routines before we begin the work of creating rules because the routines allow children to navigate the day with a sense of order, purpose, and ease. These beginning routines create the safety and boundaries the children need in order to engage in conversations about creating meaningful rules.

I also find that young children need to have at least a rudimentary understanding of what their new classroom and school year will be like before they can have meaningful thoughts about goals or the creation of rules. The way I introduce and reinforce the routines gives the children a context to draw upon in thinking both about what might be in store for the year and about what rules might be necessary.

The teacher creates the routines

Although I involve the children in many decisions about our daily life in the classroom, I create the routines myself. Empowering children is important, but we need to understand our own responsibilities as the adults in charge. In order to empower children effectively, we have to be clear about the areas we are not willing to let go of, and routines that ensure the smooth running of the day for everyone is one such area.

This is not to say that we shouldn't help children understand the reasons behind the routines. The reasons for raising your hand to talk, walking in a line through the halls, or sitting in a circle in meetings are not obvious to young children who are still egocentric in their thinking.

Sometimes I get students thinking about the reason for a routine by asking questions. "Why do you think we need to line up to get our lunch?" or "Why do we sit in a circle at meeting?" Other times I explicitly tell

Taking Care at Meeting

Everyone comes to meeting.

Bring just yourself.

Listen to each other and take turns.

Sit in your own space.

Use friendly clear voices.

Keep an eye on the person talking.

Guidelines for meetings in a K–1 classroom

children the reason for a routine. "Everybody's ideas are important. When we take turns talking, we have a chance to hear all ideas."

I have also found that children are enthralled with the idea of being connected to children everywhere. When I teach them about raising their hand to speak, for instance, I talk not only about wanting to hear everyone's ideas, but also about children all over the country learning to raise their hand to talk, just as they're doing. Suddenly children become more interested in raising their hands.

Modeling and practicing until routines are automatic

Because we can't assume that children will know what a routine should look and feel like, modeling is an indispensable step. I might ask, "Who can show me a safe way to line up for lunch?" or "Who can show me a quiet way to walk down the hall?" Everyone who wants to demonstrate gets a turn.

Recently I watched a class of children modeling how they might listen to someone who was sharing. One by one, the children had a chance to show how they would listen. Their faces and their bodies gave the message, "I get it. I can do this. I understand." I could see them almost puff up while the rest of the class watched with rapt attention. It was evident that by simply acting out respectful ways of behaving, the children not only understood what respectful behavior meant, but actually felt respectful.

The next step after modeling routines is to practice them consciously until they become automatic. I say "consciously" because getting a routine down solid is a gradual process that requires us to stop and reflect as a group, deliberately and repeatedly, on how we are doing. We think together about how well we circled up during recess this past week, about whether we're better at stopping and looking at the teacher when we hear the chime signal, about whether there seems to be a new problem in the art cleanup routine. This conscious focusing on our progress helps children remember the importance of routines, identify rough spots, and solve problems together.

Breaking down the routines: Walking through the halls

Early in the process of learning routines, I help the children by giving them more directions and breaking down complex routines into manageable parts.

For instance, during the first week of school, before we walk through the hall I remind the children with words and a gesture that others are working, so they need to "zip up their mouth and tell their feet to walk." I then lead them along in an exaggerated tiptoe to where we are going, frequently stopping to give the thumbs-up signal to let them know they're doing a great job. If the children become noisy, we stop until everyone is quiet again.

The next week, I might only make the "zip up our mouth" gesture before we begin, stopping the line again if children forget to walk quietly.

Once this step is going smoothly, I give children the challenge of walking on their own. At first I go halfway down the hall and tell them to see if they can bring the line all by themselves to where I am standing. I make sure they will be successful by going only as far as I know they can manage. I then give a thumbs-up signal and go a little farther down the hall so that they can do it again. When this is going well, I go all the way down the hall. Eventually I go out of sight.

When students are able to walk quietly in the halls without me, I know I can walk at the end of the line, and the children will know what to do. Of course they will still forget sometimes, but they understand the expectations, so getting back on track will be all the easier.

This gradual letting go of control on my part and placing it in the hands of the children is an underlying goal of all my teaching. Ultimately I want the children to be independent learners in a social setting.

The "Quiet Place"

In addition to establishing basic classroom routines such as getting quiet at the quiet signal, raising a hand to speak during meetings, circling up, and walking in a line down the hall, we need to give children a structure for comforting themselves when they're upset. In my classroom, there is a "Quiet Place" for this purpose. This is in addition to the time-out space, which I'll discuss later in this chapter. Based on ideas in Jane Nelsen's book *Positive Discipline in the Classroom*, the Quiet Place is a cozy place in the room where children can go voluntarily to be alone and help themselves feel better. (Nelsen, Lott, and Glenn, 2000)

I introduce the Quiet Place during the first week of school. As with the routines, I introduce it before we begin working on the rules because when children see that their own emotional needs will be considered, they are freer to think about the issue of classroom rules.

The "Quiet Place" in Deborah Porter's K–1 classroom

I never insist that a child go to the Quiet Place, but I frequently suggest it. The spot is especially useful to kindergartners making the transition from home to school and struggling with separation anxiety during the early weeks of school.

Alison, a young five-year-old, had a particularly hard time saying good-bye to her dad. After going through all the usual routines—blowing a kiss, waving goodbye at the window, drawing a picture for her dad—Alison was still distressed. Though upset, she knew what to do. She grabbed her stuffed animal and made a beeline to the Quiet Place. After ten minutes of cuddling with her stuffy and looking at a book, she joined the group, happily and on her own. Not that Alison wasn't sad the next day when her dad left; but she had a way to help herself feel better.

The room itself

Another important ingredient in developing community and self-control is the room itself. I set up the room to invite interaction among classmates, with tables instead of desks to work at. Eventually, the room will be equipped with a wide range of materials that encourage children to experiment and be creative.

But on the first day of school, there are only a few familiar materials out. Then, in the next few weeks, I'll carefully introduce new materials one by one, guiding children to explore the materials actively and share their discoveries with each other.

My goal in starting with a nearly empty room, however, is not just for the sake of introducing materials. It is also because right from the beginning I want to be able to say "yes" to the children more than I say "no." If the room is full of materials that the children want to use but are not yet able to manage, the first few weeks of school will be one long series of "nos":

"No, you can't knock down your building."

"Don't splatter the paint."

"No, you can't climb that high."

"No, the pattern blocks are not for catapulting."

The refrain will go on and on, punctuating every activity and framing all interactions in the negative. Seeing school as a place of restriction before one is able to see it as a place of possibilities is counter to the active participation that I want to encourage in all children.

Creating the Rules

Beginning the process: "Why do we come to school?"

It is in a refrain of "yes" that we begin the conversations that will help us frame the rules for the classroom. I begin by asking the children, "Why do we come to school?" Sometimes the first response from the children is, "You don't know?" But after some thought, children begin to articulate what they think:

"To learn things."

"To get better at making friends."

"To learn the things you need to learn to be a grown-up."

"To have fun. Fun! Fun! Fun!"

"Yeah, because you learn better when things are fun."

"So if you come to school to learn things, make friends, and have fun, what do you think our schoolwork will be this year?" I ask. Hands wave madly. I write each child's idea on easel chart paper:

"I think we will learn to read."

"I know how to read. I think I will read more books."

"We will make new friends."

"I think we will learn how to write."

"We might write stories or about stuff."

"We will get to know things."

"Yeah, like science things."

Soon, I see that we have exhausted most ideas and the children are getting antsy, so I stop this preliminary discussion to go on to other things. I don't want to rush such important work. The purpose of this first session is to set the context for children to think about their hopes and dreams for the year. I have found that young children are more thoughtful in this process if they understand precisely what we mean by "schoolwork."

Listing our most important goals: "Of all these things, what are you most hoping to do this year?"

The next day, we come back to our list of different kinds of schoolwork and reread it to see if we want to add anything. I then ask the children, "Of all these things, what are you most hoping you will get to do this year?" I tell the children to think about the question for a minute before they answer. We then go around the circle so everyone has a turn giving an answer. Those who are not ready to give an answer can simply pass for the moment. We will come back to them.

"I hope I get to build lots of different things."

"I hope I get to build giant snap cubes things."

"I hope to do puzzles."

"I hope to play on the computer."

And so forth.

Interestingly, this list of personal hopes tends to be more concrete and simpler than the children's fairly abstract ideas of what "schoolwork" might be. That's okay. It's a reflection of where children this age are in their thinking.

This list of most important hopes is a rough draft that we will come back to several times. I want the children to think carefully about this question, and as is true for all of us, their first idea is not always what they ultimately want to stick with.

Brainstorming for rules: "What rules do you think we'll need so that everyone can learn?"

The next day we begin again by rereading the list of everyone's hopes. I then say to the class, "It is important that we all get to do the things we

Part of a hopes and dreams display in a first grade classroom

I want to learn about Antarctica.
Olivia

*Some second graders'
hopes and dreams
illustrations.*

Ben hopes to get better at math.

really want to do this year. If we want to all reach our hopes and dreams, what rules do you think we will need? What will make our classroom a safe and friendly place where everyone can learn?"

Again I record the ideas:

"I think we should keep everything nice and beautiful."

"You should work hard and do your best."

"You shouldn't knock anything down."

"Fix up your mistakes."

"Don't be mean."

"You shouldn't hit."

"What about hurting kids in other ways?" I ask.

"Yeah, you shouldn't hurt anyone."

"Treat others the way you want to be treated. That's the . . . um . . . What is it?"

"The Golden Rule?" I help out with terminology.

"Yeah, the Golden Rule."

"Stay in your own space."

"When should you do that?" I ask.

"At meeting."

"What about at other times, like if you were at a table drawing?"

"Well yeah, I guess at all times."

Seeing that the children are out of ideas for now, I tell them that this list is also a rough draft and that we will look at it again later to make sure we have everything.

Grouping the rules: Place, self, each other

That night, I look over the list. At the bottom I write "place," "self," and "each other" in three different colors. The next day the class looks at the list again. I have three markers that match the colors of the words at the bottom of the chart.

If an idea for a rule was originally phrased in a negative way, I now ask the children to think about how to phrase it in a positive way.

For example, one of the ideas was "Don't be mean":

"If we aren't going to be mean, what will we do if we are really mad?" I ask.

"Nice, you have to take care in a nice way."

"Well, what about when you have a problem with someone? Is there a way you should solve the problem?"

"You gotta solve a problem in a friendly way."

This turning the negative into a positive is a critical step. So often we assume that if we say what not to do, everyone will know what to do. But that's not necessarily the case, even for adults. Stating a rule in the positive gives us all a road map to follow as we negotiate the many twists and turns of the day.

After reading through the rules, I tell the children that I notice that all the rules they came up with fit into three different and important categories. I point to the words "place," "self," and "each other" at the bottom of the chart. "Let's see if I'm right."

We read the ideas on the chart together and decide which category each idea fits into. As we decide, I bracket the idea in the color that matches the category. When we're done, I ask the children if there is a way to say a rule that covers all the ideas in each category. That way, I explain, there will be fewer ideas, and that will make them easier to remember.

Of course, the "place" category is the easiest because there is only one idea in that category. So "Keep everything looking nice and beautiful" is the rule for that category.

We then look at the category about how to treat each other. We decide that if you are treating someone the way you want to be treated, then you would be nice to others and solve problems in a friendly way. So that category is easily consolidated. The rule is "Treat others the way you want to be treated."

The last category about how to treat yourself is a little harder. The children look confused about how to consolidate all the ideas in this category into one sentence. I ask them, "If we just said 'Take care of yourself,' would all the ideas fit into that sentence?" They look doubtful, so I say, "Well, let's try." We then go through each idea to see if it fits the sentence. When everyone is satisfied that all the ideas fit, we adopt "Take care of yourself" as a rule.

The final list: The teacher adds a rule

As we read over the final draft of our rules, I tell the class that I have one more rule that I, as the teacher, think it's important to have. I tell them it's a rule that I learned from a student in my class several years ago, a rule I have never forgotten.

"Who in our room should be able to play and learn?" I ask. They stare at me as if I had just asked the most obvious question in the world.

"Everyone gets to!" one child exclaims.

"I think so, too!" I declare. "So the rule I want to add is 'Everyone gets to play and learn.' What do you think?"

Several heads nod, and one student remarks, "School wouldn't be fun if you didn't get to play."

"And you gotta learn because if you don't, when you grow up you won't know how to do stuff," adds another.

I add the last rule to our list. We end this meeting by reading over our final rules. From the wiggly bodies and hungry looks, I can tell it's time to stop and have a snack.

"Publishing" the rules

The next step in this process is to "publish" our work. In this case, "publishing" means making a display of the final rules in a prominent place in the room so that we can refer to them throughout the year. This is usually the children's first introduction to the idea of publishing their work, so I emphasize working hard to make the display beautiful.

I make sure the display reflects the children's work. Sometimes I come up with the basic design; sometimes it's a combination of their ideas and mine. But the artwork and the writing are done by the students. And because this is a "publication," I tell students they have to use correct spelling. I help them with the spelling and writing as needed.

It's important to continue linking the hopes and dreams with the rules as we use the rules throughout the year. To help us do this, each student's hope and dream is included as part of the display. This is also the children's last chance to revise these goals. I sit down with each child to write out a statement. If the child is satisfied with the statement, the child signs it, and we add the statement to the display.

Sometimes when I go through this rule-making process, I come away thinking that this task is just too hard for young children. There are years when it feels like I have to pull the ideas for rules out of the children, and often it takes several tries to get a workable list of ideas.

I have to keep reminding myself that this is a first important step in a yearlong process of learning to live in a careful and caring way. For most of the children I teach, framing rules in the positive and linking them to what we most want to accomplish is a very new way of thinking. It's no wonder this is hard for them. But it's important that I engage them in this hard work.

Above: Rules in a second grade classroom. The stars, bearing the students' names, show that the students agree to the rules.

Below: Rules in a first grade classroom. Surrounding the rules are the children's hopes and dreams.

Living with the Rules

Showing that behavior expectations matter: Going right into logical consequences

The children have articulated their goals, they've created the rules, and the rules are now on display. It's a huge accomplishment. Still, there is quite a gap between establishing behavior expectations and consistently making positive behavior choices.

To make good choices about behavior, we need to understand the rules and believe that they are meaningful. Going through the process of generating rules helps children believe this, but that's only the beginning. As teachers, we need to exert leadership in ensuring that this initial commitment is sustained even in the most challenging moments of the year.

One way we show children that the rules matter is by enforcing them. Although we still have a lot of proactive work to do, including thinking about, modeling, and role-playing how the rules might apply to different situations, I dive right into the idea of logical consequences. By doing so, I'm telling the children, "The rules we made are important, and I am committed to making them work."

Asking questions to hear children's thoughts

In discussing logical consequences, my goal is to help children see the sense in discipline. I want them to begin to understand that there is a logic and reason to why certain actions lead to certain results—why, for example, playing a game in an unsafe way might mean you can't play the game for a while.

Moreover, I want them to see that they can influence outcomes, that outcomes don't "just happen" or come from some mysterious outside source. If they want to keep playing the game, they can ensure that outcome by playing safely. When children see the role that their "self" plays, they are more likely to develop self-control.

The way I talk to children about logical consequences makes a difference to whether they'll reach this understanding. If I talk in lecture mode, allowing minimum discussion and asking questions only to solicit my predetermined right answers, children will simply try to figure out what I think is right and parrot it back to me.

On the other hand, if I ask questions because I really want to know what children think, and I invite children's ideas and reactions, they'll be more likely to think for themselves, listen to each other, and build upon each other's ideas. They'll be actively involved in making meaning, and discipline will make more sense to them.

Focusing first on the positive consequences of following rules

When I first started using the *Responsive Classroom* approach, I began the conversation about logical consequences by talking about what might happen if children did something wrong. I have since learned that just as children need to frame the rules in the positive, they also need to think about consequences in the positive so they can imagine the benefit of following the rules. So now I introduce the idea of logical consequences by having the children think about how following the rules might bring good results for them.

"We just finished making rules," I say. We read over the rules together and I continue, "These rules are important because they will help us all do the things we want to do in school. All year long we will be working on getting good at following them. I know it is not always easy to remember the rules, and we will all need to work on this. You will, I will; in fact everyone in the school will, even the principal." I want to emphasize that the rules are for grown-ups too, not just the children.

"As the teacher, it is my job to help us follow the rules. Today I want us to think about how that might look," I say. "Let's look at the first rule, the one about taking care of yourself. Can anyone imagine what would happen if you were playing on the climbing structure and really taking care to do it in a safe way?"

"You probably wouldn't get hurt."

"Yeah, and you would have more time to play."

"Do you think you would have more fun?" I ask.

"Definitely."

"If you were playing safely, would you be following the rule about taking care of yourself?"

"Yes!"

"So the consequence of playing safely is that you would have more fun and that you would get to play longer, right? Does anyone know what I mean when I say 'consequence'?"

The response to this question depends greatly on the age and sophistication of the group, but whether or not I have to fill in the blanks, the point I want to convey is that a consequence is the result of an action. I am always prepared to give more examples if children still seem at all doubtful that following our rules indeed brings positive consequences.

What happens when we don't follow the rules?

We then look at the other side of consequences: what happens when we forget the rules or choose not to follow them. This time I ask, "Can anyone imagine what might happen if you forgot to take care of yourself on the monkey bars?"

Immediately there is a chorus of ideas and gruesome possibilities. Young children are well schooled in accidents and love to describe them in gory detail. I try not to dwell too long on this, moving quickly to my point.

"That's right, when you forget to take care of yourself, a consequence could be that you hurt yourself," I say. "Probably if you hurt yourself you would learn to be more careful next time, but that seems like a hard way to learn about taking care of yourself. If I am your teacher, and I see you doing something dangerous but just let you play until you hurt yourself, I wouldn't be doing my job."

I then go on to talk about how it might make more sense for me to tell them they can't use the monkey bars for a while. In this way I introduce the idea of a logical consequence and make it easier for everyone to accept the idea. Although getting off the monkey bars might be upsetting, our conversation has helped children see that it's a helpful and fair way to handle the situation. Later, when a monkey bar situation arises, and I know it will, we will have a common understanding to draw upon as we deal with it.

In this conversation, there are several key points that I want to be sure the children understand:

- Stopping misbehavior helps keep everyone safe.

- Everybody breaks the rules sometimes because everyone is human, and humans are not perfect.

- A logical consequence can help you remember the rules and fix things before you get hurt, before you ruin a friendship, or before you do something that can't be fixed.

- A logical consequence is one that makes sense because it relates directly to the situation at hand. (To illustrate the point, I also give examples of consequences that don't make sense.)

- Logical consequences are part of the important work of school.

Introducing Three Types of Logical Consequences

It's not enough to leave the conversation here. Although we might have to come back to it later when everyone is fresh, the next thing I do is to share with students the three types of logical consequences as described in Chapter Three. These types—time-out, loss of privilege, and "you break it, you fix it"—are easy even for young children to understand.

Time-out

Of the three types, I usually introduce time-out first. I bring a chair labeled "time-out chair" to the meeting area and tell the children that I want to introduce them to a friend of mine.

Explaining the purpose of time-out

"Now why would I call the time-out chair a friend?" I ask.

"Because it helps you when you do something wrong," reports an experienced six-year-old.

"Right, this chair can help you," I affirm. "We just made some rules that will help us do the things we most hope to do this year. But I know that it is hard to remember to follow the rules all the time. To get better, we all need to work at it. When you forget to follow the rules, it is my job as a teacher to help you remember, and one way I might do that is by telling you to take a time-out."

I pause a bit, then continue. "If you forget to follow our rules, and I tell you to take a time-out, what do you think I would expect you to do?"

Again the experienced six-year-old is ready with the information. "We would have to go and sit in the time-out chair."

I show children the designated spot for the chair. Time-out goes much more smoothly when the children know just where to go. Because we want children to rejoin the group as soon as possible, the time-out spot should be close enough to the activity of the room for children to see what is going on in the classroom. This is especially true of young children, who easily forget about things not immediately near them.

I get the children to consider what they might do when they're in the time-out chair to help themselves calm down and regain self-control. I say, "Sometimes it helps me to think about a favorite place that makes me feel calm when I am trying to get back in control. Would that help you?" The children agree that it would.

I prompt the children to name additional ways they personally might help themselves regain self-control. We all have different ways of coaching ourselves back on track. My intention here is to encourage the children to develop, within limits, their own strategies.

Discussing coming back from time-out

After I'm sure the children understand the purpose of time-out, I talk about coming back from it. "Who is the best person to know if you are ready to come back?" I ask.

Most children answer that the teacher is.

"I might be able to make a good guess," I respond, "but who will know for sure?"

Often children themselves are the best judges of whether they are ready to return. I believe children can make that decision responsibly if they are given the opportunity to learn what being "ready" means. Sharing and thinking about what being calm and in control feels like, looks like, and sounds like will be part of the ongoing reflective work of the year.

The first time a student goes to time-out, I always let the child decide when to come back. Sometimes children sit for barely a second, but that's okay as long as they come back ready to contribute positively. However, if a child comes back after seconds, only to resume the same antics, I step in. I tell the child to go back to time-out and "I'll decide this time when you can come back."

Over and over throughout the year, my message to the children is that when they choose not to take care, I will. Not taking care is never an option.

Modeling time-out

Now we're ready to model how to use time-out. Again I lead with a question: "If you need a time-out, how do you think you should go?" Several children show their ideas by walking to the chair and sitting down. Whenever we do this modeling, it is the children who need time-out the least who are most eager to try out the chair.

I ask another question: "If someone needs to take a time-out, how will we all help that person do what he or she needs to do? What is our job when someone is in time-out?"

"To leave them alone?"

I nod.

"Not talk to them?"

"Not distract them?"

Often these are tentative answers because for many children the idea that they, too, have a job to do when a classmate goes to time-out has never occurred to them.

We then watch as a few volunteers demonstrate that job. The modeling session ends when everyone who wants to model has had a chance to and the group has seen good ways to walk to, stay in, and return from time-out, as well as good ways to leave the person in time-out alone.

Demystifying time-out

I know that all children will need to take a time-out at some point. That's why, as we begin to use the strategy for real, I make sure that any child who is particularly reluctant to use time-out has an opportunity to experience it sooner rather than later.

My goal is to demystify time-out as much as possible. Some children may fear time-out because they see it as "getting in trouble." If these children experience time-out and see that they can survive it, they will be more likely to make good use of this self-control strategy throughout the year.

What to Call Time-Out

Even though I make no apologies for using time-out, I sometimes avoid using the term "time-out" with children because for many of them, the term has negative connotations. Perhaps they've seen time-out used elsewhere as a threat or as a punishment. It's often just too hard to shake these preconceptions.

For this reason, many teachers call time-out by a different name. Some have their students help choose one. Some names I've heard are "taking a break"; "chilling out"; and "rest and return."

Whatever name is chosen, it should be a short, simple description of time-out and should not work against the goals of time-out. The term "sit and think," for instance, can easily become "Sit there until you've thought about what you did." It assumes that children need to think about what they did in order to change their behavior.

I know that when I've made a mistake or begun to lose control, usually what I need isn't to think about what I did, but to break out of a negative cycle by disengaging for a moment. That's why I like the term "taking a break." I think it's a neutral term that clearly reflects the purpose of time-out.

Sometimes demystifying time-out requires working with parents before that first time-out experience, so that all the adults can be on the same side in supporting the child.

Laura was a child who strove for perfection. She took any small correction as a sign of some major failure on her part. It was easy to see that her first time-out would not be easy. I had talked with all the children's families about the purpose of time-out and how we use it in our classroom, which made it easier to work with Laura's parents to plan how we would react when Laura needed a time-out. We acknowledged that the sooner she had her first time-out, the sooner she might relax about it.

Within a few days the opportunity arose at meeting time when Laura leaned over to whisper a comment to her friend in the middle of someone's sharing. I quietly told her to take a time-out, and she quietly walked to the chair. The only thing betraying her feelings was her bright red face. After a little while she returned to the meeting, and we all went on with the business of the day.

Later, however, when her mother asked about her day, Laura cried, "This is the worst day of my life."

When her mother asked why, the whole story tumbled out with great emotion and declarations of how unfair it all was. Although her mother responded with compassion, she also asked Laura how Evan might have felt when she whispered in the middle of his sharing.

"Bad," Laura responded.

"If I were Evan, I also might have thought you weren't interested," said her mom.

"Oh."

"So what else happened today? Was it all bad?"

"No!" And on Laura went, happily describing other events of the day.

In Laura's case, her own high expectations made her mistakes particularly painful for her. It was probably unavoidable that her first time-out felt so bad. If we had protected her from her mistakes or tiptoed around her, the message would have been that she was better than the other students or that she was not strong enough to take responsibility for her mistakes. Either way, Laura would have felt more inadequate in the long run.

What happened instead was that she lived through time-out and realized that it wasn't the end of the world. She also learned that she was more resilient than she had thought. The next time Laura went to time-out, it wasn't nearly as difficult.

What about the negative connotations of time-out?

Many teachers and parents worry about the negative effects of time-out. Won't it make children feel isolated? Singled out? Humiliated?

There's no question that time-out has frequently been misunderstood and misused. Using the strategy well requires care and practice. However, I don't believe we should abandon a good teaching technique just because it's challenging to use.

If used well, time-out does not have to be punitive or humiliating. It can be used in the most matter-of-fact way as a time to regroup. (See Chapter Three for guidelines for using time-out effectively.)

Children must know that when things aren't going well, the teacher will step in and take charge. Sometimes this means that a child will need to leave the group temporarily. I make no apologies for this. Teachers who skirt around this responsibility risk losing their authority as the teacher.

As for concerns that time-out might make children feel bad, it's important to keep in mind that these are times when children are losing their self-control and not functioning well in the group. They will sometimes feel bad about this. While I would never want to humiliate them, I also know I can't and shouldn't try to take away the bad feelings. Often our feelings of regret are the very thing that drives us to change our behavior the next time.

Because my goal is not to make children feel worse, but to help them pull themselves together, I don't wait until a child is fully out of control before I step in. Instead, I use time-out when a child is just beginning to lose it. This is before the child has lost face in the group and before I've lost my patience. It's at this point that time-out is most effective. Like those grooves on the side of the highway, it's a gentle nudge to get us back on track before we barrel off the road.

Loss of privilege

As useful a tool as time-out is, it's only one possible response to misbehavior. When teachers rely too heavily on it, they may overlook other possibilities that might be far more effective in certain situations. Once time-out is in place, I introduce loss of privilege to students.

As with our other work around behavior expectations, we begin with a conversation. I use the following five-step format in this discussion:

- Presenting a common situation to children

- Discussing which rule has been broken

- Thinking together about several possible consequences that would make sense

- Doing controlled role-plays of several possibilities

- Reflecting on the role-play

I find that these conversations require me to really pay attention. I want to stretch and broaden children's thinking. But the temperament, age, and sophistication of each year's particular group of children significantly affect the tone and depth of the discussion. What follows is one possible way the discussion could go, but it is never the same from year to year. If needed, I scale back and simplify. In all cases, though, it's important for the children to feel that their comments in these discussions are taken seriously.

A common situation

"Yesterday we talked about time-out," I begin. "Who can remind us of what we talked about?" I want to establish a connection between time-out and the other kinds of logical consequences we're about to discuss.

"If you are bad, you might have to go and sit in the time-out chair for a while," one student says.

"We did talk about times when you might need to sit in the time-out chair, but is it because you are bad or because you need to remember to follow our rules?"

"Because you need to remember."

"I think so, too. You might need help to follow the rules. Everyone will sometimes. But that doesn't mean you are bad." It's important to keep correcting children's misconceptions that making mistakes is "being bad" or that time-out is a punishment.

Then I introduce the new ideas. "There are some other ways that a teacher might help you follow the rules, and we are going to talk about that today." I decide to present a scenario about unsafe play.

"Remember when we talked about forgetting to play safely on the climbing structure? What was it that we said might happen if you forgot to play safely?"

"You might get hurt?"

"Right. I wonder how our rules would be working if people were not playing safely on the climbing structure?"

"Not very good?" says a tentative five-year-old.

"Yeah, the rules are supposed to help you be safe," relates a more confident six.

"Yeah, and if you get hurt you wouldn't have fun," adds another child.

These children have a pretty good handle on the general purpose of rules.

Which rule has been broken?

Now I push the children to think more specifically. "So let's look at our rules again," I say, then read through the list. "If you were not playing safely on the climbing structure, which rule do you think you would be breaking?"

"Not taking care of yourself?" one student suggests.

"Yeah, because you might hurt yourself," another confirms.

"And that wouldn't be taking care of yourself," yet another student chimes in.

"That makes sense. Does everyone agree that you would be forgetting the rule to take care of yourself?"

Several heads nod. I go on. "What about the other rules? What about treating others the way you want to be treated?"

"Well, I think that you might be breaking that one," a student says, "because you might hurt someone else if you weren't playing safely, and you wouldn't want someone to hurt you."

This prompts animated conversation, in which children share one story after another of siblings and friends knocking them over, falling on them, or kicking them because of careless play. After several tales, I pull the children back to the work at hand.

"It sounds like everyone agrees that if you weren't playing on our structure safely, you would also be breaking the Golden Rule. How about the other two rules, 'Keep everything looking nice and beautiful' and 'Everyone gets to play and learn'?"

There is silence while everyone thinks. Then one kindergartner raises his hand.

"Well, I wouldn't want to play on the structure if it was too wild. So I wouldn't get to play."

"So it sounds like unsafe play would be breaking the 'Everyone gets to play and learn' rule, too."

Because our classroom rules are general guidelines and not prescribed behavior for specific situations, figuring out which rule has been broken in a particular incident is not as easy as it might seem. Does running through the room mean you are not taking care of yourself? Or does it mean not taking care of others? If you bump into something and knock it over, are you not taking care of the space or not taking care of other people?

Questions like these always arise as the children try to make sense of the rules. It's critically important to refer back to the rules when misbehavior occurs so children will keep seeing how rules help keep the classroom safe and friendly. But in the end, which actual rule the children might pick is not as important as the discussion of the rules themselves.

What are some consequences that would make sense?

The children still seem engaged, so we continue.

"So if someone isn't playing safely on the structure, what do you think should happen?" I ask.

The children are full of ideas:

"Send them to the principal's office."

"Call their parents."

"Make them stay in for recess for the rest of the week."

These initial ideas are always extreme. It's not that children are blood-thirsty for harsh punishment; it's that following rules is something they really care about. My job now is to lead them toward more tempered thinking without discouraging their dedication to rule following.

So, after affirming their ideas, I say, "When I have to choose a consequence to help someone, I think about it this way. See if it makes sense to you." I show a chart of the three kinds of logical consequences and briefly explain the two new ones—loss of privilege and "you break it, you fix it."

"If you forgot to play safely on the structure, would it be a situation where you broke something you needed to fix?" Several heads shake no.

"Would it be a situation where you weren't careful in how you used something?" Heads nod yes.

"Yeah, I think so too. So does that mean loss of privilege is what fits as a consequence?"

The children think again and I am mindful of the time. I don't want to keep these young children sitting too long, but we are at an important place in the discussion. Finally someone nods his head and then others follow.

I ask why loss of privilege would be a good consequence, and someone pipes up, "Well, if you don't use something carefully, you shouldn't get to use it. That's what my mom says."

"Do you think you should never get to use it again?"

"No, just for a little while."

"That makes sense," I say. "So if you forget to play safely on the structure, a teacher might say that you need to get off the structure for, say, the rest of the recess time?"

"Yeah."

A logical consequence is a way to stop misbehavior and restore safety and order. It is not a punishment. But understanding this does not come automatically for anyone, child or adult. This discussion is only the beginning of helping these children understand.

I know we will need to keep sorting and discussing and thinking together as we confront the many varied instances of classroom misbehavior and conflicts during the year ahead. Again, how deeply I go into the thinking behind logical consequences during these discussions throughout the year depends on the age and maturity of the children.

As for today's conversation, I stop here to give children a break so they can move their bodies and chat amongst themselves.

Controlled role-playing

After coming back from the break, our next step is to get a little taste of what the logical consequence we decided on might look like in the moment. Although I sometimes use modeling for this, more typically I use role-playing because usually there are many possible ways for students to act when a logical consequence is applied, and role-playing allows for that complexity.

I control the role-play by taking the key role. I need to be in the center of the action, steering so that all the behaviors acted out stay within a positive and safe range.

"Okay, we decided that if you play unsafely on the structure, a logical consequence would be that you would have to get off the structure," I begin. "Let's imagine I'm playing on the structure and forget what we said about no jumping off the fire pole. The teacher sees this and says, 'That's not safe. You need to get off the structure.' I'm having a good time on the structure but I know I need to listen to the teacher and pay attention to our rules. What do you think I should do?"

"Get off."

"How do you think I might feel about that?"

"Bad."

"Mad."

"Yes, I would probably feel mad and bad," I affirm. "What could I do about those feelings?"

"You could go to the Quiet Place."

"You could see if a friend could play with you."

"You could go play another game."

"If I did these things, would I be following our rules?" I ask.

"Yeah," several kids say.

"Would I never get to play on the structure again?" It's important to remind children that a loss of privilege is not forever.

"No," one child responds with a smile.

"Let's see how handling my feelings might look. I'm going to try the suggestion to go play another game. Who wants to take the part of the teacher?" Hands wave madly. Everyone wants to be the teacher. I choose one child to say the teacher's line, and we act out the scene. I get off the structure and join a jump-rope game.

Reflecting on the scene

It's important that the role-playing doesn't stop there. Before role-playing other suggestions, it's critical to reflect on what just happened. This reflection informs the teacher about what the children understand and can guide the teacher in planning what should come next. More important, though, it's often upon reflection that children take a big step forward in understanding the connection between actions and the results they bring.

I open the reflection by simply asking the group, "What did you notice about what just happened?"

"You got off the structure."

"And?"

"Well, you still got to play, just not on the structure," a student responds.

"You knew what to do," another points out.

"How about the teacher, how do you think the teacher felt?" I ask.

"Upset that you weren't following the rules."

"And?"

The children hesitate. Taking this new perspective is hard for them.

Finally one child says, "I think the teacher might feel worried that someone was going to get hurt."

"She might feel mad that you weren't doing what you were supposed to be doing," another adds.

"Do you think she might also feel impressed that you were able to go off and find something else to do that was safe?" I ask.

Heads nod, with some relief.

"I think if I were the teacher here, I might feel all of these things," I add.

This has been a very substantive conversation. I don't believe children truly understand the idea of logical consequences until they encounter them in action, but our discussions begin the process. Depending on children's energy and attention span, I might role-play another one of the suggestions or I might save that for another day.

"You break it, you fix it"

Within the next few days, I present a situation for which the third type of logical consequence—"you break it, you fix it"—would be appropriate. I use the same five-step conversation format as before, but because we have already had a good introduction to the idea of logical consequences, this conversation does not have to be quite so involved.

I present the situation where someone knocks over someone else's building by mistake. Again, the class examines together which rule was broken, determining that "treat others the way you want to be treated" was the main one, although several children also point out that maybe the rule "keep everything nice and beautiful" was broken, too.

As before, we look at the chart to figure out what kind of consequence would make sense. Because I know this group of children is capable of fairly sophisticated thinking, I push them to consider why neither time-out nor loss of privilege would work.

"Well, the building wouldn't get fixed," an astute child responds.

"So what do you think should happen?" I ask.

"The person should fix the building," another child proposes.

"What if they don't know how it went?" objects a third.

"That would be a problem," I agree, and turn to the class for ideas for solving this problem.

"Well, you could ask the person that was making the building."

"Maybe you could go tell the person that you knocked it over and see what they want you to do."

"Okay, let's see how this might look." I take the children into role-playing. I play the student who built something with pattern blocks. Aisha is the child who accidentally knocks the building over, and Gabe is the teacher.

Aisha smiles self-consciously as she gently knocks my building down.

Gabe says, "Aisha, you should fix that building."

"Oh, okay," responds Aisha. She says to me, "I didn't mean to knock your building over. I'll fix it."

I reply, "Okay, let me show you how it goes."

After we put the building to rights, I ask the children what they noticed.

"The building got fixed!" one exclaims. Then, as we did before, the class talks about how each character might have felt in the scenario.

I then push a little further. "When you make a mistake, do you think you could do a fix-up without the teacher's help?"

"Yeah!" a confident child exclaims. And so we pick new players, Tyrin and Ramon, and act out the scene again, this time without the teacher intervention. When the role-play is finished, I ask the class what they noticed. They point out that the children "didn't need a teacher to help" and "the building still got fixed."

"Yesterday we talked about working independently," I say, reminding children of another conversation from the day before. "Do you think Ramon was being independent when he fixed the building without a teacher to remind him?"

Several heads nod, and I leave the discussion there for the moment. We will act out more scenarios in the weeks to come, so that the children will have a lot of practice in "you break it, you fix it."

Guidelines for Using Logical Consequences

By teaching routines, generating the rules, and teaching logical consequences this way, I set the stage for creating a caring learning community. But I know that simply setting the stage does not automatically mean the play will go well.

In the next few weeks, I can expect a rigorous testing of the limits. Children's eyes will all be on me to see how I handle classroom situations. They'll be looking to see if I really mean all that stuff I said during the early days of school, for they know, rightly, that actions speak louder than words.

Teaching positive behavior effectively means handling each situation from a position of interest and caring for the child. It requires us to approach momentary struggles not as adversaries of the children, but as their partners. It requires us to greet problems without assigning blame or making excuses, but with a readiness to find solutions together. I know from my own experience that this is an area that needs ongoing attention.

The following are some guidelines for implementing logical consequences that I have gathered from teachers who have used this approach effectively.

Stop the behavior before you act

As presented in Chapter Three, a teacher's first responsibility is to stop the misbehavior. In addition to keeping children safe, telling children to stop gives teachers a chance to think about what consequence would make sense rather than trying to come up with one in the heat of the moment. We don't always need to decide on a logical consequence right then and there.

Much better to give ourselves some time, if needed, to collect our thoughts. We can let children know we'll get back to them with a fair and reasonable way to handle the situation. When we act out of frustration, we often decide on an overly harsh consequence that defeats our goal of helping the child develop self-control.

I remember once at Morning Meeting being interrupted for the umpteenth time. Out of utter frustration, I proclaimed that the next person who interrupted would have to stay in for recess. Of course the next person to interrupt was the shyest child in the class who needed all the encouragement she could get to speak up in meeting. Imposing such a consequence on this child only served to silence her further. The fact that the consequence was illogical—because staying in from recess had no relevance to interrupting—made the matter worse.

Analyze the problem

Once you've stopped the behavior, you'll have time to think through what the best action might be. Here are two questions to answer in deciding on an appropriate consequence:

What has to be restored to order?

If a child spills paint, a clean working area is what needs to be restored. Therefore cleaning up the paint ("you break it, you fix it") might be a fitting consequence. If a child refuses to take turns in a game, a respect for the rules of the game is what needs to be restored, and so being removed from the game for a while (loss of privilege) might be appropriate. If a child is moving too fast and furiously through the room, the child needs to return to a calmer and quieter state. A time-out might be what's needed.

What does the child need to learn?

I recall the time the principal of my school marched one of the class's more impulsive boys back to our room after lunch. The principal announced that the boy had shown atrocious lunchroom manners and, as a consequence, would have to eat alone for the rest of the week.

Later, when I asked the principal what he hoped the boy would learn by eating alone, he responded, "To use better manners at lunch." Pointing out that the child might not know what good table manners were, I offered to eat with the boy and give him lessons for the rest of the week.

During the course of the lessons I discovered that the boy rarely ate dinner with any adult, which might have explained his behavior. At the end of the week, the child ate passably better—I've learned you can't expect perfect table manners from six-year-olds—and was happy to rejoin his classmates in the cafeteria.

Know the child—understand what's behind the behavior

Using logical consequences consistently is not the same as using them uniformly. The point of using logical consequences is to resolve the problem in a way that makes sense for the child and to restore positive behavior as quickly as possible, not to carry out the letter of the law. That means teachers need to read each situation and try to understand where the child is coming from. Consequences very quickly become illogical and, potentially, counterproductive when we try to apply them uniformly to all situations.

In our school, there is a rule that any student who physically hurts another has to go home for the rest of the day. One year, there was a kindergartner in my class who was having a particularly hard time adjusting to school. Out of the blue one day, he started hitting other children. He had discovered the hitting rule and was using it to get himself sent home.

Needless to say, we did not send him home. Instead, after conferring with his parents, I sat down with the child to ask if the reason he was hitting others was because he wanted to go home. When he said yes, I simply told him we weren't going to send him home, and the hitting stopped. We then worked on other ways to help him adjust to school.

Even if you decide that a consequence is in order, knowing what was behind the child's behavior allows you to handle the incident in the most appropriate way. One year, a six-year-old in my class, excited at getting a fancy new pencil, wrote his name on the back of a bus seat without thinking. Once he saw his mistake, he tried to correct it by using his spit to wash off the seat. The bus driver saw this and gave him a ticket for defacing the bus. Terrified of getting in trouble, the child, rather than owning up to what happened, began to lie about the whole incident.

When the principal and I finally unraveled the problem, I told the student of a time when I was just learning how to write my name and wrote it all over my mother's bedsheet with a red crayon. I let him know we all make mistakes. The principal then offered to help him wash off the bus seat properly. The child still got the bus ticket, but it was the washing of the seat that helped him fix his mistake in an honest and restorative way.

Have some common "bottom line" consequences ready

Although the goal is to fit the consequence to the situation, there are instances in which a preset response is warranted. Most often these involve issues of immediate safety. When children run through the hall and know that it is not safe, I respond by taking away the privilege of walking through the halls independently for a short period. When children go out of bounds on the playground, they temporarily lose the freedom to play on their own. These are what I call my bottom line consequences, and the children know they can count on these being used without discussion or negotiation.

Avoid lecturing: Have faith that the consequence will do the job

A consequence doesn't need to be accompanied by a lecture to be effective. If in choosing a consequence we follow the three Rs—the consequence is directly related to the child's action, is realistic, and is respectful of the child—then the consequence itself should do the job.

If we lecture or show anger, our good intentions will most likely be undone and our actions will feel like a punishment to the children. The children will focus on defending themselves rather than adjusting their behavior. I know that if I feel the urge to lecture or make accusations, it's a good clue that I've waited too long to use a logical consequence and am feeling either ineffective or so angry that I want revenge.

The less said, the better

If children know the rules, often no words need to be spoken at all. I once saw a teacher remind a child to put a toy away. The teacher said, "Toys don't come to meeting. Put it away." Quickly the child put the toy in his pocket, but just as quickly he pulled it out again. The teacher responded by simply holding his hand out. The child put the toy in his hand, and the teacher put the toy away. Not a word was said during this second interaction, and the meeting was not interrupted a second time.

Look to a buddy teacher for help

When I first started teaching, it was the norm for teachers to close their classroom door and go it alone. Thankfully, that's changing. Increasingly, teachers are encouraged to help each other, and for good reason. Many schools have a buddy teacher system, in which pairs of teachers agree ahead of time to lend each other a hand in using time-out (see Chapter Three for more information). But having a buddy teacher also opens up informal options for handling problems.

Recently, I was able to help a colleague resolve a sticky situation. At lunch this second-third grade teacher was expressing frustration because she wanted to take her class out to study a wooded area near the school that afternoon, but one child had behaved so badly all morning that the teacher felt she couldn't allow the child to go.

The choices, she thought, were to send the girl to the principal's office for the rest of the day while the class was out or to cancel the woodland study for the whole class. Both choices seemed too harsh. So I offered to take the child for the rest of the day, which would allow the class to go to the woods.

The girl came into my room with all the work she had been avoiding that morning. Surprisingly, she got right down to work and stayed focused with a minimum of check-ins from me. Meanwhile, the children in my class kept stopping to marvel at her work.

This was a child who felt very unsure of herself when it came to school-work, and suddenly her work was being greatly admired. As she left the room at the end of the day, she said, "I can hardly wait to show Ms. Carson what I did." Meanwhile, Ms. Carson's class got to have its afternoon in the woods.

Live by what you decide

For logical consequences to be effective, we have to mean what we say and say what we mean. When we set a standard and then fail to follow through on it, our actions say to the children that we don't think they can really meet the standard or that the standard doesn't really matter. In any case, both our credibility and the children's faith in themselves become eroded.

There's no question that it takes courage to stop a kickball game that has become mean-spirited, refuse to go on with a lesson when children aren't listening, or stand up to a parent who is unhappy about a consequence you chose. But as long as they're reasonable, these firm and decisive actions are exactly what children so often need and appreciate in the long run.

Communicating with Families about
Responsive Classroom Discipline

I find that the more that families understand the *Responsive Classroom* approach to discipline, the more effectively we can work together to help their child. It's important to begin communicating with families early on, then continue throughout the year. Here's a sample letter that I send to families as soon as the class has created its rules:

Dear Families,

Well, we are off to a great start! The children come in each day with enthusiasm and are busy learning all about their new classroom, their new classmates, and some of the routines in our day. It was great to see so many of you at the open house. The kids did a great job being the tour guides.

One of the important jobs of the first few weeks of school is for the children to make classroom rules together. To make the rules, the children had to first think about what they hoped to do in school, then figure out the kind of rules that would help us all accomplish those hopes. The rules that the children created are:

- Keep everything looking nice and beautiful.
- Treat others the way you want to be treated.
- Take care of yourself.
- Everyone gets to play and learn.

These rules are broad guidelines that we will work on following throughout the year. This will take lots of attention and practice. We expect mistakes and, as I told the children, it is not the mistake but how you learn to fix it that counts. My job, as the teacher, is to help children learn to fix their mistakes as well as to understand the consequences of their actions. If our ultimate goal is for children to become independent, lifelong learners, then it is important that they learn how to make good decisions in settling differences and taking care of mistakes in constructive ways.

You can support your child by reading over these rules and talking about them. It's important that your child knows your expectations, too.

Sincerely,
Deborah Porter

Many years ago a teacher at my school decided to take a group of children caroling. I joined in to help. This was our first trip out into the neighborhood after having moved the school to this new location the previous summer, and even though we would have very little time to practice, we very much wanted to sing our best for our new neighbors. The teacher in charge made it clear to the children that due to these circumstances, choosing to participate in the caroling meant choosing both to sing and act their best without reminders.

With a group of enthusiastic singers, we began our practice. As we started in on "Jingle Bells," one fourth grader began singing at the top of his lungs, "Jingle bells, Batman smells, Robin laid an egg." I quietly went over and sent him back to his classroom, saying he would not be taking part in the caroling. No discussion, no explanation.

That night, I got an irate phone call from the boy's father, who felt I was being far too harsh. I explained that his son knew ahead of time what kind of behavior the situation demanded. Still the father would not be put off. He felt his child deserved another chance. Finally I agreed to talk to his son the next day.

When the boy and I met, I asked the boy if he knew what he had done wrong. He said he did. I then asked if he remembered what Ms. Doris had said would happen if any child couldn't do what was expected. He knew this as well. I then wondered aloud if he was disappointed in himself for not behaving in a way that would allow him to go caroling, and he nodded silently.

Continuing, I asked if he thought it would be fair if I let him go anyway since he was feeling so bad. Surprisingly, he said no. I agreed that I couldn't let him go. "But does that mean you can't sing with the school ever again?" I asked. He smiled and shook his head. I told him that in a week, a student would be leaving the school and we would be singing the traditional good-bye song to her. "I'll be leading that singing. I would love to have you help me and in that way show all the kids what a good job singing you can do," I said. He agreed to the plan and went back to his classroom.

That night I got another call from the boy's dad. "I don't know what you said to him, and I still think he should be able to go caroling. But he seemed happy about the solution, so I guess it's fine," he said.

Keep a sense of humor

Developing self-control is serious work, and we all need a little comic relief sometimes. Amidst all the talk of rules and logical consequences, I am not above being silly or unpredictable on occasion. At cleanup time, for instance, I might put on Groucho Marx glasses and tell the children I am the "Cleanup Inspector" and will be inspecting how well they've done their jobs. I make a big show of walking around the room, examining each space, asking who is responsible for that area. If the space is clean, I congratulate the children by telling them to pat themselves on the back. If it is not clean, I tell them to do a quick fix-up and then to pat themselves on the back. I only need to do the Groucho Marx routine a few times before the room is always clean the first time around.

Reconnect with the child

The use of logical consequences is a positive way to help children get back on course, a way to restore order and relationships. When this involves a child leaving the room, either for time-out in a buddy teacher's room or to go to the principal's office, it's important that the child have a chance to reconnect and come to resolution with the classroom teacher upon returning. That means we must take the time to go get the child, talk about what happened, and agree on what needs to be done differently in the future.

Without this step, the air will be thick with questions and uncertainty when the child returns to the room. The child worries, "Does my teacher still like me? Do the other kids like me?" The teacher wonders, "Is this child really ready to be here? Is the child going to blow up again?" Instead of resolution there is tension all around.

Try again if you make a mistake

One thing I like about an approach to teaching that recognizes that everyone makes mistakes is that it allows me to gracefully make them as well. If we thought we had to be perfect teachers, our job would overwhelm and defeat us. Like the children, we will make mistakes, and like the children, we need to be able to go back and try again. Being able to admit to mistakes and then fix them is what brings authenticity to the work I do.

Sometimes when my patience has worn thin, I find myself issuing drastic threats like "There will be no recess if the room is not cleaned up in five minutes." Immediately, I stop and say to the children, "Erase that. Let me try again. As soon as we are all cleaned up, we will go outside. The quicker we clean, the more time we will have to play outside." Other times I simply apologize for saying or doing something that is not in keeping with our rules.

Hold fast to rules in the most challenging moments of the year

No matter how carefully we lay the groundwork for a positive classroom community, there are times in the year that try our patience and test our goodwill. For me it is usually the end of February, a time when the beautiful snows of January turn slushy and dirty. Soggy mittens litter the radiator, wet boots make puddles outside the classroom door. Sorting out whose sock, mitten, or boot is whose delays our outside play and postpones our silent reading work, making the rest of the day a rush. An air of irritability hangs about the corners of the room, and I, in my rush to get to everything and my worry over the progress of certain students, am often the main source of it.

These bleak moments of the year are a critical time for preserving the integrity of the rules. After all, if the rules don't help safeguard us when our spirits are low, what good are they? From experience, I know that if I allow myself to ignore the rules when my temper is short, the spirit of our classroom community will nose-dive. I've learned that sometimes I can change the weather of the classroom by simply stopping my own behavior and taking stock of the rules.

One recent February day, as I gathered the children at the rug for our cleanup meeting, I realized how tired I was. It had been a full morning: learning subtraction, writing poems for the first time, taking a few Running Records on the first grade readers. I felt impatient with the children who poked along. I was about to erupt into yet another tirade about how it was time to stop work and come to the meeting when I happened to glance over at the rules. "Take care of yourself," I read. I took a deep breath and rang the bell for quiet. I told the class that I needed a quick rest and that I would take one while they came to the meeting rug. "I just need a minute. When I open my eyes, I expect everyone to be ready for our cleanup meeting."

I went and sat at the meeting area and closed my eyes. Quietly and slowly I counted to sixty, while just as quietly all the children put down what they were doing and came to join me. When I opened my eyes, everyone was assembled and I really did feel refreshed enough to go on in a positive way with the rest of the morning.

Later in the day, after recess, when the mittens and boots began piling up again, I could look at the mess with renewed energy. Playfully I told the children that we were going to have a contest. They would see if they could get all their things off and put away in five minutes. If they could, they would win the contest; if they couldn't, their stuff would win. I set the timer, saying, "On your mark, get set, go!" As the children raced to beat their own stuff, I reminded myself that February would end. I was relieved that this time I was able to stay in control of myself, and confident that my patience would be tried many more times before the end of the year.

The fact that we take such care in teaching and practicing positive behavior does not prevent difficult times or short tempers, but it does help us deal with these frustrations with a little grace. I knew that on another day, I might not be able to keep myself in check, that I might make mistakes and, like the children, have to do fix-ups. But as I watched the children assemble on the rug for story, all having won the "contest," I also knew that I was in the best of company and looked forward to the work we had ahead of us.

Rules as a Prelude to Problem-Solving

During the first weeks of school, so much of the children's attention is on the teacher. But as they go about the business of figuring us out, testing what we believe in and seeing how we react to different situations, they are also busy making friends, learning about their school, and seeing how they themselves fit into the whole picture. It's hard to put your finger on the exact moment when "the first weeks" of school move into the rest of the year, but it certainly comes with the children's discovery of each other. Suddenly I'm realizing that instead of testing my limits, the children are testing each other and reporting back to me every detail and result they find.

"Teacher, Zachary butt me!" "Teacher, Emily says I can't sit next to her!" "Teacher, Lifang won't let me be the mother. I never get to be the mother!" "Teacher, Alden is using all the wheels and I don't have any!"

If we allow ourselves to become drawn into every dispute and apply first aid to every hurt feeling, our firm and consistent enforcement of rules can easily turn into a search and rescue mission. It's tempting to jump in to settle disputes, defend the underdog, erase hurt feelings. It is our job to care, and certainly these are a few of the ways we do that each day. However, we get ourselves into trouble when we confuse rescue with education.

Teaching positive behavior must lead to the teaching of problem-solving if we are serious about giving children the tools they need to work things out for themselves. After teaching behavior expectations and enforcing them through the use of logical consequences, it's critical that I give children a repertoire of problem-solving techniques, from whole-class problem-solving meetings for situations involving all students to conflict resolution strategies for problems involving two or three students. (For more information on problem-solving strategies, see Appendix A and *Solving Thorny Behavior Problems* by Caltha Crowe.)

Our classroom rules serve as a guide for our problem-solving, regardless of the type of problem or the technique we choose to address it. If one of our rules is to treat others as we want to be treated, we now ask ourselves, "How can we solve this problem so that we're living by that rule?" If we've agreed to the rule "Take care of yourself," we will now ask whether the proposed solution to a problem would allow us all to take care of ourselves.

Finally, our work on practicing positive behavior helps create an expectation that problems in our community will be solved, and it leads children to feel confident that they can be the ones to solve them. Of course I'll need to reinforce this expectation continually, and I'll need to keep nurturing children's belief in their abilities, but the foundation we laid in creating rules together, applying those rules to day-to-day life, and using logical consequences makes this work go so much more smoothly.

WORKS CITED

Crowe, Caltha. (2009). *Solving Thorny Behavior Problems: How Teachers and Students Can Work Together*. Turners Falls, MA: Northeast Foundation for Children, Inc.

Nelsen, Jane, Lott, Lynn, and Glenn, H. Stephen. (2000). *Positive Discipline in the Classroom* (3rd ed., rev.). Roseville, CA: Prima Publishing.

Grades 3–5

By the time third grade rolls around, most students can rattle off a long list of things that shouldn't be done in school. With three years of classroom experience behind them, they've seen a wide range of approaches to discipline and many examples of students' behavior problems interfering with learning. Most come away from these experiences with a clear understanding of the forbiddens: no fighting, yelling, interrupting, running, pushing, cutting in line, chewing gum, and on and on. These, to them, are the rules in school.

But ask third graders what they should do instead of fighting, yelling, interrupting, etc., and most of them will say something vague such as "be good." Ask them what "being good" means, and they're likely to say simply that it means avoiding being bad, or at least avoiding being caught being bad. What's missing is the ability to name behaviors that are specific and positive.

The flip side of this, of course, is that the students equate breaking rules with "being bad." Unfortunately, when children this age repeatedly see themselves as being "bad" when they break a rule, they're likely to grow discouraged in their attempt to become "good."

The good news is that students in these grades are capable of changing the way they look at rules. Still highly receptive to adult guidance and eager to participate in group conversations, they welcome the idea of co-creating rules that are based on their own and their classmates' goals for the year.

They appreciate the modeling, role-playing, and discussions that clarify exactly what it looks like, sounds like, and feels like to follow the rules.

Over and over I've watched students in these grades dramatically change how they view rules as a result of the process described in this book. While they will still break the rules or complain about following them from time to time, they develop a deeper understanding of why rules are important. They come to see how the rules help them personally and how the rules help them coexist peacefully and productively with others.

Achieving this positive vision of rules, however, takes time, careful planning, and patience. And it all begins from the first day of school.

Setting the Tone from Day One

Third, fourth, and fifth graders walk into school on the first day every bit as excited and nervous as their teachers. Although more savvy than their early elementary counterparts, these students still rely on the adults in charge to set the tone for the school year.

Questions like "Will we have homework this year?" "Do we get recess every day?" "Where should we put our things?" "Will we have lots of tests?" and "What are the rules?" are the test questions for the unspoken thoughts and fears of the students: Will I be safe here? Will I be able to do the work? Does the teacher like to have fun? Is this classroom ours or just the teacher's? Does the teacher like kids?

The task of creating a positive learning environment for all of the students rests with the teacher. Students in these grades need to know from day one that this is a classroom where they'll feel safe and respected. They need to know that the teacher is organized and in control. They need to know that there are predictable routines and procedures.

Modeling and practicing basic routines

On the first day of school, I spend time modeling and practicing procedures for basic routines such as lining up, coming to the meeting circle, taking out and putting away materials, going to recess, and using the signal for quiet.

We also take time to establish guidelines for group discussions. I tell students that we'll be meeting together as a whole group a lot this year, and we need to make sure these meetings run smoothly. We then brainstorm together to come up with guidelines that will allow everyone to feel comfortable participating and allow everyone's ideas to be heard. (See the discussion and photos of meeting guidelines in Chapter One.) It's essential to have these basic routines and meeting guidelines in place before opening the discussion of our goals for the year.

Articulating Goals

My own goals: "How do I want this class to be?"

Before talking with students about their learning goals for the year, I always ask myself how I want the class to be: What's my hope for how we'll treat each other? For how students will approach their learning? For what we'll accomplish this year? It's critical that I answer these questions earnestly, because it's my positive vision that will set the tone for students to articulate their goals earnestly.

A third grader's illustration of her goal for the school year: "I hope to learn how to read in cursive."

It's also critical that my vision be clear and easy to communicate to students and families: "This year I hope everyone will feel safe about trying things that feel hard," for example. Or "My hope this year is that everyone will enjoy coming to school and working hard." Or "My goal this year is

From a display of hopes and dreams in a third grade class. The first illustration says, "I hope to do lots of times tables in third grade."

for all students to feel excited about learning and be comfortable working at their own pace." Then, when I ask students about their goals, I open the conversation by expressing mine.

Posing the question to students: "What are your hopes and dreams for the year?"

When I ask the students about their goals, I often refer to them as "hopes and dreams." I might ask, "What are your hopes and dreams for learning this year?" or "What would you like to accomplish this school year? For example, do you want to get better at reading, or learn to do harder math problems, or write lots of stories?"

There are a variety of ways for children to share their responses. Often I simply gather the students in a circle and invite them to give their answers. Some students will name three or four hopes right away; others will wait, gathering ideas as they listen to their more vocal classmates. I write down all of the students' ideas on a chart pad.

Next I ask each student to choose, from all the hopes they named, a single most important hope. Again, I often simply ask students to think about this question for a few minutes while sitting in the circle. Those ready to share their responses do so, and I record each response on the chart with the child's name next to it. Those who aren't ready to share right away will have an opportunity to do so the next day.

Other times I turn this naming of the most important goal into a writing assignment, to be done during school that day or as a homework assignment that night. The next day, students bring their writing to the circle and share it with the class. Again, I record everyone's response on a chart pad.

From a fourth grade class's hopes and dreams display

Whatever the process, we end up with a chart of each child's most important hope and dream for the year. We post the chart in a prominent place in the room, usually near the meeting area where we'll be able to refer back to it frequently throughout the year.

This public sharing of goals conveys the message that everyone's goals are important. It also sets the stage for the idea that we'll all be helping one another achieve our goals and that we have rules in our classroom for this purpose.

"To make new friends": The importance of social goals

The first time I did this process, it was with a class of fourth graders. I didn't know what to expect, but one thing I felt sure about was that students should name goals related to academics. Otherwise, how would we work on the goal within a classroom context?

So when Joshua said that he would like to make some friends, I was tempted to redirect him. But when I stopped to think about it, I realized, "He does need friends." In fact, of all the things Joshua needed to learn at school that year, figuring out how to make friends was probably the most important. Since then I've come to understand that social goals are every bit as worthy as academic ones, and that students are remarkably astute at choosing a goal that's right for them.

Here's a partial list of goals from that fourth grade class:

- Ms. B. hopes that students will find learning fun and will want to come to school every day.

- Chris hopes that he will get better at writing.

- Juan hopes that he will get an A in math.

When a Student Doesn't Have a "Hope or Dream"

Occasionally, a student will have difficulty thinking of a single goal or won't even want to do the activity. Possibly the child has moved a lot and has learned that it can be painful to invest in a classroom when the possibility of another move looms. Or maybe the child has yet to see a goal realized. Ironically, it's perhaps these students who need this process more than anyone.

I try the following to help students who are unable or reluctant to name a goal:

Change the language

Some children find the phrase "hopes and dreams" to be threatening or unfamiliar. With one third grader, I changed the phrase to "hopes, dreams, and wishes." The word "wishes" seemed more accessible to her. Using the more straightforward language of "goal" or "learning goal" may also be helpful for some children.

Have the student think about a shorter period

Often, thinking about what we'd like to accomplish in the next month or two is easier than thinking about what we'd like to accomplish in the next year. With one fifth grader, I changed the question to "What's your hope for the month of September?"

- Marta hopes to read a long chapter book this year during DEAR.

- Katelyn wants to learn fractions and decimals.

- Pha hopes to improve his art skills.

- Shanice hopes to learn to use the Internet.

- Joshua would like to make some new friends.

Involving families: "What's one hope you have for your child this year?"

During the first week of school, I send a letter home to families asking two questions: "What do you think was the most important thing your child accomplished last year?" and "What would you like to see your child accomplish this year?" (See sample letter on page 159.) The students will have just done the hopes and dreams activity, so I also suggest in the letter that families ask their child about the goal the child named, as a way to start a conversation about this topic at home.

Moving from Goals to Rules

When teachers and students speak publicly of their hopes for the year, a sense of group identity emerges, and children begin to feel ownership of the classroom. The next step is to help students see the connection between their hopes and their classroom rules.

"What rules will we need to help all of us reach our goals?"

I always discuss this question as a whole group even if students wrote about their hopes individually, because it's so important for children to hear one another's ideas about what rules are needed.

I begin by saying, "Now that we've named our hopes and dreams for this year, let's talk about how to make them come true. Classroom rules are one thing that can help. What rule might help you meet your goal or help others meet theirs?"

If this is the first time a particular group of students is doing this activity, I know they'll name a litany of negatively framed statements: "Don't be mean"; "Don't yell"; "Don't copy other people's work"; "Don't interrupt people." This happens simply because children (and adults) are used to thinking of rules as what they shouldn't do. I'm prepared to help students turn their don'ts into dos:

Dear Families,

We're off to a great year! One of the first activities in our class this year is thinking about what our most important goals for this school year are. I invite you to join this activity by sharing your goals for your child. Please take a few minutes to answer these questions:

1. What do you think was the most important thing your child accomplished last year?

2. What would you like to see your child accomplish this year?

This week in school I asked the children to name a learning goal for themselves for this school year. The children wrote down their goal and then illustrated it. You may want to ask your child about the goal that she or he named.

I look forward to talking with you from time to time this year about your goals for your child and his or her progress toward meeting them.

Please send this letter back with your child by September 5.

Thank you.

Sincerely,

"If Juan hopes to get an A in math this year, what can he do to try to make that happen?" I ask.

"I could do all my work," Juan says.

I write Juan's idea on the chart pad. "What could we do to help Juan?"

"We could not bug him when he's working," Chris suggests.

"So if we're not going to bug Juan, what are we going to do?"

"We could let him work 'til he's done."

I write "Let people finish their work" on the chart. Then I say, "I notice we have several people who want to learn new skills. What rules might help these people meet their goals?"

Marta, who had told the class she hopes to read a long chapter book this year, says, "I will need to read when it's quiet."

"So what would you like people to do, Marta?" I ask.

"Respect DEAR time and read quietly."

I write "Respect DEAR time" on the chart. "Let's talk about Pha wanting to improve his art skills. What kind of help might Pha need?"

We continue in the same fashion, talking about what would help different students realize their hopes until we've generated a long list of positively stated rules.

Rules in a third grade classroom (left)
and a fifth grade classroom (right)

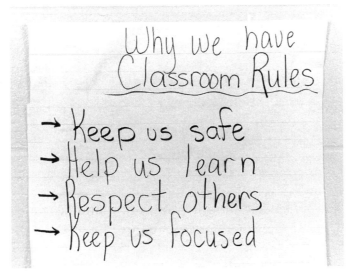

In this fourth grade class, the children made a poster to remind themselves of the reasons for having rules.

I'm always struck by how well this exercise suits children this age. Eight-to ten-year-olds have a developing sense of personal and community responsibility, a keen interest in fairness, and generally like to have expectations spelled out. A discussion of classroom rules usually proves engaging and fruitful for children this age.

Getting it down to a few global rules

After taking a break, the class goes on to the next step, synthesizing all of the ideas for classroom rules into a few broad ones. There are a number of ways to do this. Many teachers simply ask children to look at the long list of ideas and see if they notice any common themes. I've also seen teachers cut the chart sheet of ideas into strips so there's one rule per strip, then ask the children to place the related strips together.

One method I've used is to group a few of the rules into categories and ask the students to do the same with the rest of the rules. I bring out a chart that I started. It lists just a handful of the many rules we came up with the day before, divided into three columns:

Invite others to play. **Use nice words.**	**Take care of basketballs.** **Take care of art supplies.**	**Respect DEAR time.** **Let people finish their work.**

Though I haven't labeled the columns, they represent three fundamental categories that classroom rules tend to fall into:

- Treatment of self and others (first column)

- Treatment of personal and communal property (second column)

- Treatment of the learning environment (third column)

The first two categories are familiar and easy for most children to understand. The third is a category not often addressed overtly in upper elementary classrooms, yet it's an issue critical to students' success in school.

Picture a typical scene of students taking a test. One by one, the students finish until only a few children are still working. Often it's these last few children who most need quiet in order to finish. Yet the children who finished early are up, moving about, whispering or talking to others who've finished, and giving no thought to the needs of classmates who are still working. While the early finishers might argue that they aren't specifically bothering those who are still working, they need to be taught to take care of the general atmosphere of the room by being quiet.

The same goes for all other times during school. Children need to be taught why and how they should be quiet during quiet times, participate fairly in activities, use established cleanup routines, respect the quiet signal, and so forth, so that all class members have the kind of environment they need in order to work at their best. In making this an overt category of rules that's equal to the more familiar two, my intention is to draw children's attention to this area of behavior and encourage active discussion about it.

Now, showing children the chart, I invite them to finish the columns and think of appropriate labels for them:

"What do you notice about the rules in the first column?" I ask.

"They talk about how we should be friends."

"Do we have any other rules that could be grouped with them?"

" 'Be nice to everybody' could," someone suggests.

I add that rule to the column.

" 'Invite others to lunch' fits with those, too," another student says.

I add that idea to the chart as well. The first column now looks like this:

> **Invite others to play.**
>
> **Use nice words with others.**
>
> **Be nice to everybody.**
>
> **Invite others to lunch.**

When the class is satisfied that no other rules fit into this group, I say, "These rules are all very important, but it's hard to remember a long list of rules. It might be easier if we could make one rule that says what all these rules say. How might we say that one rule?"

"How about 'Be friendly with everybody'?" Taylor asks.

I write this on the chart pad. "What are some other ideas?"

"Remember that people should get respect?" Cara asks tentatively.

I write that on the chart pad, too. "Other ideas?"

There are one or two other suggestions. The class then looks over the ideas and, taking bits and pieces from each one, decides that "Respect and

take care of everybody" would be a good label for column one. This becomes our first classroom rule.

We go through the same process for column two, then column three, until we've come up with three global rules that cover all the specific rules generated the day before. The three are:

- Respect and take care of everybody.

- Use materials carefully.

- Let everybody learn.

While this process of synthesizing the rules can feel time-consuming, there's great value in taking children through it. Thinking together about how various rules are related leads the group to a shared understanding of what the rules really mean. Over the course of the year, children will need to make countless decisions big and small as they navigate classroom life. This shared understanding will be critical if the rules are to be truly useful for guiding them in making these decisions in responsible ways.

Interactive Modeling and Role-Playing

Like adults, children don't follow the rules all the time, even when they have the best intentions. However, children will be more likely to follow the rules if we teach them how. Two techniques that I've used successfully for this teaching are interactive modeling and role-playing.

But first, teachers need to ask themselves a critical question.

"How will I know if students are following the rules?"

This might seem like a silly question at first. "Children are following the rules if no rules are being broken," one might respond. Or, "They're following the rules if they're doing what I ask when I ask."

But timely compliance is not a measure of how well children are learning to think for themselves and make positive behavior choices.

The purpose of rules is more than to create order and compliance. It's to help students learn about and practice keeping themselves and each other safe physically and emotionally as they pursue their goals, grow, make mistakes, and try again. To get beyond the idea of compliance, we need to consider what the classroom might specifically look, sound, and feel like if students are regularly using the rules to guide their behavior.

Asking children the question

A few days after the children create their final classroom rules, I open a conversation:

"We've had our new rules for a few days now," I say. "To help us follow our rules, I think we should look at them one at a time and talk about what each rule might look like, sound like, and feel like." I take out a chart with these headings written at the top. "Let's start with 'Respect and take care of everybody.'"

"So if we're respecting and taking care of everybody, what are we doing or saying?" I ask.

Envisioning specific, positive actions and words like this is not something the children are used to doing. They think for almost a minute.

Finally, Joshua says, "When we're at recess, we don't keep kids out of the games." Reverting back to what not to do is common. I need to keep pushing children to envision the positives.

"If we're not going to keep kids out of games, what would you like to see happen?"

"When I have to go out to recess late, I want to play basketball instead of watching," Joshua replies.

"What could you do to make that happen?"

"Ask to play with the kids?"

I write, "Ask to play or participate" and "Ask for help" under "Sounds like" on the chart. "What might others do to take care of someone who wants to play?"

Pha says, "Let kids join in."

I write, "Let others join in" on the chart under "Looks like." "It sounds like this is an easy thing to figure out on the basketball court," I continue, "but I'm wondering if there might be a time when this is really hard to do."

Marta says, "When we play tetherball, we only play with two kids. What if someone else wants to play?"

"We could take turns playing the winner, but what if we don't want to?" Katelyn joins the discussion.

I write, "Take turns" under "Looks like" on the chart, then say, "I hear that there might be two hard things about making sure everybody gets to play. There might not be a spot for the person, and we might not feel like giving up a turn to let someone else play."

Here is an opportunity to focus proactively on taking another person's perspective and developing empathy, something that usually isn't addressed until after a conflict arises. "Let's say you're watching a game," I say. "Imagine that the game looks like it's a lot of fun, but you're too shy to ask to play and there isn't another way for you to join in. How would you feel?"

"I would feel ignored." "I would feel left out."

"It would still be hard to share a turn," Juan persists. He's clearly identifying that this might be a hard thing for him personally to do.

"It might be hard," I concede, "but our rule says that we need to respect and take care of everybody and it sounds like taking turns might be part of that. I know it's not always easy to take turns when you want to keep playing. I think we'll talk about this many times this year."

I know this will be a challenging issue for this group, and I make a mental note that Juan, for one, will need me to acknowledge his efforts whenever he does relinquish a turn or invite others to join a game.

For now I continue with our conversation. "Now let's flip the situation around. How would it feel if someone noticed you were standing by the side and asked you to play?"

"It would make me feel like I count for something."

"So you'd feel important?"

"Yeah, and like I belong."

I write, "I count for something" and "I belong" under "Feels like" on the chart. "Anybody else have an idea?"

"It would make me feel like I have friends."

I add, "I have friends" under "Feels like." "Let's talk a little about what this rule would look like inside the school, either in the classroom or in other places in the building."

By the end of this conversation, our chart for our first rule looks like this:

Respect and take care of everybody

Looks like (our actions):	Sounds like (our words, voice, tone):	Feels like (how we might feel):
Let others join in (recess, class, cafeteria).	Ask to play or participate.	I count for something.
Take turns.	Ask for help.	I belong.
Walk quietly in the hallway.	Ask questions that show we are listening.	I have friends.
Listen when others speak.	Use words that encourage.	
Raise your hand to speak after others are done speaking.	Speak kindly.	

In the same way, the class talks through the specific applications of the other two rules.

Some observers of the "looks like, sounds like, feels like" exercise have wondered whether it merely asks students to restate the specific rules that the teacher asked them to consolidate. But the exercise is more than that. Coming after the students have had a few days to begin putting the rules into action, it helps students reflect on this early practice and consolidate what they've experienced so far.

Students are now able to be even more specific than before in stating desirable behaviors. They're able to apply the general rules to areas of the classroom and the school that they didn't think of earlier. Further, this second round of conversation helps students see more clearly how the three rules relate to one another and how our words and actions affect how people feel.

Interactive modeling: Seeing expected behaviors in action

After we've articulated these clear visions of positive behaviors, the students and I move into interactive modeling so that children can see their visions brought to life.

I've seen interactive modeling used effectively to teach everything from how to carry a chair to how to put slides into a microscope. Modeling sessions can be quite simple and yet make an impression on students.

Here's a typical interactive modeling session I did with fourth graders:

"Each morning, we will be coming together in a circle on this rug for our Morning Meeting," I begin. "Some days, we will need to bring our chairs. We need to be able to do this quickly and safely. Watch me carefully as I carry a chair to the rug."

I lift the chair by its back posts, just below the seatback. Holding the chair in front of my midsection with the chair legs several inches above the floor, I walk carefully, looking to either side of the chair as I move. Then I place the chair gently on the outer edge of the rug, putting the front legs down first.

"What did you notice?" I ask after I finish.

"You walked with the chair."

"You didn't carry it over your head."

"So how did I carry it?" I ask.

"In front of you, so the legs were up off the floor, too."

"You held the chair by the back part."

I ask the student who made this last remark to come and point to where he saw me carrying the chair. Then more children name other things they saw me do.

Teachers as Constant Role Models

Whether we like it or not, we are always a personal model of rule-following for our students, who seldom miss gossiping, facial expressions, or other signs of disrespect among adults. The fact that students often misread even innocent interactions born of frustration as acts of intentional disrespect just makes it all the more important that we keep watching how our words and body language might be coming across.

Third through fifth graders, in particular, with their emerging sense of justice, will quickly pick up on a system in which adults are somehow held to lower expectations of conduct than students. If the rules we created with students are based on respect for all and by all, then our actions must match this expectation, or we will undermine our own efforts to teach children to live by the rules.

"You were looking around at the floor and furniture while you were carrying the chair."

"Why do you think I did that?" I ask.

"I think you were trying to be careful not to bump into stuff."

"That's right. Did anyone notice anything about how I put the chair down?"

"You put the chair near the end of the rug."

"And how did I put the chair down? Was there a loud noise?"

"It was quiet."

Next, I invite student volunteers to demonstrate this way of carrying a chair safely. Once again, their classmates name the safe, positive behaviors that were used.

The modeling session ends with my issuing a challenge to the class: to work over the next two weeks on moving the chairs safely and quickly. I'll be watching, I say, to see if they can move the chairs faster and faster without sacrificing safety. Our target will be to move all our chairs to the meeting area safely in less than two minutes.

Role-playing more complex social situations

Throughout the year but especially during the early weeks of school, I also use role-playing to teach behavior expectations. Rather than teaching students one prescribed way to do something, role-playing asks them to make some decisions about how to solve a social problem.

Role-playing can be enormously beneficial in teaching children how to handle their own problems and in helping them develop the verbal and non-verbal interpersonal skills critical to effective problem-solving. Note that the kind of role-playing I describe here is used before a problem happens. The purpose is to give students a repertoire of positive responses to situations that might come up in real life.

For example, a situation that elementary students often encounter is how to share materials. Especially among nine-year-olds, who sometimes focus to an extreme on issues of fairness, debates about sharing can often deteriorate into complete work shutdowns.

One fourth grade teacher that I've worked with uses role-playing to cut down on the number of such crises:

"We've been working in pairs for two weeks now," the teacher says to the class. "On Monday, we will begin to work in groups of four during social studies to make some maps. Working with a group of four can be lots of fun—you'll have lots of good ideas to share. But it can also be hard figuring out how to share materials. Today we're going to role-play some ways to behave when a conflict comes up about sharing materials in your small group."

The teacher pretends to make a map. "Imagine that I'm working on a map in a small group. We're all using the materials that the teacher gave us. One student in my group, let's call her Carla, wants to make a bigger map than the rest of us and wants extra cardboard and papier-mâché."

The teacher pauses and points to the class guidelines. She says, "Our guidelines say 'Let everybody learn.' How can we share our materials so everyone can do their best learning?"

The teacher gives the students a few minutes to think about this dilemma. She asks for ideas and charts the ones that offer positive solutions, in keeping with the class rules:

- The group could talk about what materials each person needs before they divide them up. If it looks like they will need more materials, they can talk to the teacher.

- There could be a job of materials manager that rotates during different projects. The materials manager decides how to divide the materials.

- Carla could ask other groups if they have extra materials that she could use.

The teacher points to the first suggestion on the list. "Let's do a role-play using this suggestion," she says. She lets the students know that she'll play Carla for the first role-play and chooses three volunteers from the class to be the other three students. The four actors confer for a moment about their lines and then act out the scene.

After they finish the scene, the teacher asks the audience to share their observations.

When a New Student Joins the Class

Integrating new students into the process of creating and applying classroom rules can be tricky, especially in schools with high transition rates. But if you've involved students in establishing rules and have devoted time to helping students learn how to make positive behavior choices, you'll have built the necessary foundation for easing new students into the group.

Ask a new student to name a goal for the year just as the other students did. Add this goal to the "hopes and dreams" display. Explain to the new student that the classroom rules were created to help everybody meet their goals and ask the new student which of the rules might help make her goal a reality. Later ask the rest of the class to explain what each of the classroom rules looks like, sounds like, and feels like. They may even be able to do some modeling and role-playing of the rules for their new classmate.

If you know in advance that a new student will be arriving, hold a discussion with the class beforehand. Talk about how it might feel scary, lonely, or confusing to be a new student. Ask students what they can do to make the new student feel comfortable and welcomed.

"What did you notice about Carla's words and voice tone?" she asks, to get the conversation going.

"She was calm," one student says.

"Yeah, she just said what she needed and didn't get all demanding about it."

"And what about the rest of the group members? How did they behave?" she asks.

"They stayed calm, too."

"They figured out if they'd have enough stuff and then made a plan to ask the teacher."

"How do you think everyone felt?"

"Like it wasn't a big deal."

"They could get their work done."

After everyone has had a chance to share their observations, the teacher points to the second item on the list of suggestions and asks for four new volunteers to role-play this suggestion. This time, a student will play Carla, with the teacher's coaching.

When the students finish acting out the second scene, the teacher again asks the class what facial expressions, body language, words, and tone of voice they noticed in the actors. Not only does she want students to see what the various solutions for sharing these materials might look like, but she wants them to become aware of the effect that nuances in verbal and nonverbal signals have on people.

The role-playing session ends when all the suggested solutions have been acted out. Importantly, there is no ultimate decision on which solution is "best" or "most fair." The point of role-playing is not to teach students one right way to solve a problem, but to help students see that problems usually have several possible solutions. The goal is for students to become more flexible in their thinking, more confident that they can solve their own problems, and more aware of how the rules they generated relate to the complex life of the classroom.

Using Language to Support the Rules

Careful use of teacher language is obviously crucial in the rule-creation, interactive modeling, and role-playing conversations during the early weeks of school. But it's also crucial in those quick two- or three-sentence interchanges about children's behavior that take place dozens of times in a school day. In these interchanges, I find it helpful to think of the three categories of teacher language: reinforcing, reminding, and redirecting.

Reinforcing language: Easier to encourage desirable behavior than discourage undesirable behavior

One thing I've learned in working with children is that it's far easier to get them to do what we want than to get them to stop doing what we don't want. In other words, instead of mostly pointing out times when students did something wrong, it's more productive to mostly acknowledge times when they did something right.

Ultimately we want children to notice their own attempts at positive behavior—this self-noticing leads to an internal willingness to honor the rules—but letting them know that we noticed is a first step.

"Gregory, I noticed you welcomed Adam into the basketball game," I might say as Gregory walks past me when the class comes in from recess.

To a small group I might say, "This group figured out a way to share the materials. How did you do it?"

Or, after the class assembles for Morning Meeting, I might remark, "It took only one-and-a-half minutes to set up our chairs for meeting. Everyone did it safely."

I purposely avoid making general statements that imply personal judgment, such as "Good job!" "You're great!" or "I love that!" when I acknowledge positive behavior. Instead, I name specific behaviors that I saw. Rather than saying to children "I'm happy that you're doing what I want you to do," I want to name specific positive behaviors and reinforce the idea that their behavior is helpful to themselves and the entire community.

Reminding language: A quick conversation before problems arise

I use reminding language to do just that: to remind students of the behavior expectations and established procedures before students veer off track.

Sometimes this means a quick review of the rules before students begin an activity. For example, before students launch into an art project that requires the use of some specialty scissors, I say, "Who remembers what we said yesterday about where and how we're to use these specialty scissors?"

"We can use them at our desks or at the art cart," says Pha, the art enthusiast. "We have to be standing still or sitting at our desk."

"Yes. And who can remind us about how these scissors will be stored?"

"We decided to put them away with the sharp points down," Diana says.

I ask Austin, our art cart helper this week, to pass out the scissors. While he's doing that, I turn to the class. "As you're creating the cover for your math notebook, you may want to exchange scissors with a classmate in your group. What's a safe way to pass scissors?"

"We should close the blades and pass them so that we're holding the blades."

This whole conversation, which took little more than a minute, will mean a smoother work session. As the students work, I'll watch them carefully so I can acknowledge the specific positive efforts that I see.

I also use reminding language when I see students about to go off track. When Danielle begins to put her scissors away with the points facing up, I say, "Danielle, do you remember what we said about how to put the scissors away?"

"Oh yeah, um, put them with the points down?"

"That's right. Do you remember why?"

"So we won't get hurt with the sharp points when we get a pair of scissors?"

"That's it exactly."

Redirecting language: Bringing children back to the expected behavior

I use redirecting language when a student has just gone off track and all that is needed to help them get back on course is a clear redirection. I tell the student firmly to stop the behavior and exactly what to do differently.

For example, during the activity using the specialty scissors, I see Malcolm waving the scissors around. "Malcolm, stop," I say. "Put the scissors down." When Malcolm puts the scissors down, I may check in with him to see if he needs a review of the procedures for safe and careful use of the scissors. Or it may be clear that the firm redirection is all that he needed. Either way, I might follow up by saying, "Let's see, what shapes did you cut with your scissors?" to bring the focus back to the project work.

When I use redirecting language, I make sure my voice remains firm but kind. I steadfastly believe that all children are good, even when they've made bad choices, which helps me to maintain my kindness. I also know that children don't need to be shamed to change their ways, so there's no reason to make children feel bad about their mistakes. Granted, in the moment of frustration, it's easy to lose my cool, but if I remind myself to separate the deed from the doer, I stand a greater chance of treating the child with respect even if I dislike the child's behavior.

Introducing Logical Consequences to Children

The rules have been created. Routines and procedures have been established. I have talked with students often about how to take care of each other, the classroom materials, and the learning environment and I've acknowledged their positive actions. Behavior problems seem manageable. This is amazing. Should I expect the year to continue without a bump? No.

Children will break the rules. They will forget, become unsure, and test limits. I know that my proactive strategies—everything from establishing goals, to modeling and role-playing, to using careful teacher language— have built a strong foundation for a caring learning community. But now I must follow up with effective reactive strategies, most importantly the use of logical consequences to teach children to take responsibility for their actions when they do misbehave.

Empathy for rule breakers: Justifications of a traffic violator

Every year—indeed every month and every week—I find I need to stop and remember that I, too, am a rule breaker. My rationale for speeding, parking in no-parking zones, and committing other traffic violations, for example, comes easily and self-righteously when I'm behind the wheel. Remembering the justifications I give for these violations helps me have empathy for children who break rules. That empathy is what must be in place before I can deal justly and effectively with children's rule breaking.

I know I'm not alone among adults in bending rules and laws when there is "justification" for doing so. Children do the same. Here's a comparison of teachers and third, fourth, and fifth graders talking about their rule breaking:

Teachers (talking with one another at lunch about speeding)	Students (explaining their behavior)
"We were running behind to begin with and then the baby threw up on me as we were walking out the door and I needed to change, which put me fifteen minutes behind schedule. I was so late for school that I drove like a crazy woman to get here on time."	On running in the hall: "I had to stay in at recess to finish my work and the team was waiting to play kickball with me, so I wanted to get there as fast as I could."
"The speed limit on Route 495 is sixty-five. I do seventy-five and people still pass me like the wind. So I go seventy-five or even faster. It's dangerous if you don't keep up with the flow of traffic."	On jumping up to slap the top of the door jamb when the class is trying to move the line quickly and smoothly through the doorway: "All the guys on the basketball team do this. It's how we keep fresh for the game."

> "The speed limit on 495 is sixty-five miles per hour? I thought it was higher. I drive seventy-five on that road, too. I need to pay closer attention to the posted limits."

> **On using restricted materials without getting permission:** "I thought it was okay to use these paints. I didn't know we couldn't."

> "I don't need to worry about getting to school late. I drive the back road, and I can drive as fast as I want because there are never any cops there."

> **On taking an extra dessert in the cafeteria:** "The woman who usually does the desserts wasn't there today, so I thought it would be okay."

> "Thirty-five miles per hour is ridiculous for that road anyway. The limit should be at least fifty."

> **On copying someone else's answer on a test:** "It wasn't a fair question anyway! You said there wouldn't be trick questions."

As these examples illustrate, adults and children alike break rules for many reasons. Sometimes we don't know the rule or we forget the rule. Sometimes we have a "good" reason, a mitigating circumstance of some sort, to break a rule. Often we break a rule because we see everyone else doing it. We even break rules because we can, because we know no one will catch us. We may break a rule because we think the rule is unfair or makes no sense. Finally, for some of us, it can simply feel good to break a rule.

As a teacher, I remind myself that following the rules can be very hard for children. This doesn't mean, however, that I shouldn't hold children accountable for their actions. In fact, it's in holding them accountable, with empathy for where they're coming from and faith that they can choose a better way, that I can teach them ethical decision making.

Beginning the discussion: "Why do we break rules?"

I introduce the idea of logical consequences to students by gathering them in a circle and exploring why people break rules.

"We've made our rules and we've been practicing following them," I begin. "I notice more and more every day how hard people are working to pay attention to the rules. But I know that there will still be times when we'll forget the rules or do something in a split second before we've even had a chance to think. What are the hardest rules to follow?"

"It's hard for me to be quiet in the library," Bonita says right away.

"I have a hard time sharing the art materials," Ian confesses.

The children are glad for the chance to tell me which rules are troublesome.

"What makes these two rules hard to follow?"

"There's really neat stuff in the library, like new books and computers. I just want to talk about it," says Bonita.

"And when I get going on an art project," Ian explains, "I don't like people to bother me and ask to take things that I might need later. It's just hard."

The conversation continues as the children share hard rules from home and school. A theme emerges. Often rules are hard to follow, it seems, because the children lack self-control and have a tendency to be self-centered, considering only their personal needs. This is fairly standard for children this age, but it's still helpful for me to hear the specifics in these children's examples. I remind myself to be aware of their self-centered tendencies and to acknowledge their efforts to consider each other's needs.

After a while I turn the talk to instances of deliberate rule breaking even when the rule isn't hard to follow. I share an example of a time I chose to break a rule, then ask children why we do that kind of thing.

"Maybe there's no one watching," Nick says. "Sometimes when there's no one in the hall, you can run and slide on the slippery floor."

"Sometimes when the bell rings at recess and the kids are having fun, they don't want to come in and they stay on the playground, so I stay too," says Laurel.

"So sometimes kids don't follow the rules because they see that other kids aren't following the rules. Is that what you're saying?"

"Yeah, it happened last week on the playground and the teacher was mad," Laurel answers.

The students continue to share instances of deliberate rule breaking. I'm struck by their honesty and enlightened by how familiar they are with the ins and outs of rules.

Getting to the positive: "How does it feel when you do follow the rules?"

I decide to dive into a discussion of the feelings that accompany breaking and following rules. I begin with breaking, although ultimately I want to arrive at reflecting on the positive feelings that come with using the rules as guideposts for behavior.

"Think about a rule you chose not to follow one time," I say. "Remember what you were doing? Think about what that felt like." After a pause, I say, "Who would like to share what you felt that time?"

One child says he felt scared that he might get caught. Another offers that she was worried. Then one student says, "Most of the time when I break rules, I get worried. But one time I felt good, like I had power."

"What kind of power did you have?" I ask.

"I cooked my mom a birthday cake, and she was so happy that she didn't get mad that I used the oven," he explains. "But I promised not to do it again."

I continue. "Now think about a time when you followed a rule, even when it was hard for you."

"One time these kids were bragging about how they wrote stuff on the bathroom walls, and they were, like, daring each other to do it. I didn't do it though," Marta shares.

"Because you remembered the rule about taking care of our environment?" I ask. Marta nods.

"How did you feel about that?"

"I felt good that I remembered the rule without anyone telling me," says Marta.

"So when you work to follow a rule, you might feel good inside, like you're in charge of yourself," I say. "When students are not in control of themselves or not taking responsibility to follow the rules, it is the job of the teacher to help those students get back to acting responsibly. One way of helping students do this is called logical consequences." The conversation now turns to the three types of logical consequences and how they can help students to get back on track when they're not following the rules.

Loss of privilege

"How many of you have ever heard about logical consequences?" I ask. Several students raise their hands.

"Last year, if we didn't treat the books or art cart the right way, we weren't allowed to use them for awhile," Mee shares.

"That sounds like something called 'loss of privilege,'" I say. It doesn't matter to me which of the three types of logical consequences we begin with. Since Mee happened to bring up loss of privilege, I go with that one.

"So if someone misuses one of our classroom materials, they may need to wait awhile before they can use it again. Why do you think they'd need to wait?"

"So they'll learn a lesson," someone says quickly.

"What do you mean by that?"

"So they'll think twice next time before misusing it."

"That's one way of putting it," I say. "But what I want everyone to know is that telling people they have to wait isn't to punish them. It's to help them remember the right way to use the material. Sometimes the teacher might show them the right way again if that's needed, or they might make a plan with the teacher for how they can remember the right way the next time."

I pause to let this sink in. Then I continue, "Which one of our rules does this logical consequence seem to apply to?" The children look at the rules chart and hands go up.

"Use materials carefully."

"Yes, this will probably apply most often to that rule. It may also apply to how we work with others and how we act in all places in this school." I describe a situation in which a student loses a special job for a week because she didn't do it responsibly.

When I ask whether anyone can think of other situations in which loss of privilege might make sense, Emily brings up the example of two students fighting over a game. "They could lose playing the game for a while or maybe they could lose playing together," she says.

The class then talks about how the two students could work out rules for playing the game fairly so they wouldn't get mad at each other. If a situation like this happened in this class, I assure the students that the two children would be allowed to go back to playing the game together eventually, once it seemed likely that they could play the game in a friendly way.

Satisfied that the class understands loss of privilege fairly well, I move on to another type of logical consequence.

"You break it, you fix it"

"Another kind of logical consequence is 'you break it, you fix it,'" I say. "This consequence could help with all of our rules. Maybe someone makes a mess in the room or breaks someone else's things. That student may need to fix those situations. Can anyone think of a time in school when they needed to fix something?"

"Last week I spilled some paint on the floor in the art room and I stayed after class to clean it up."

"That's a good example. Does anyone have another example?"

Aubrey tells about a time when a boy accidentally stamped designs all over her half-done origami because he thought it was a piece of scrap paper. The boy got a new sheet of origami paper and folded it up to the point where she had left off, and gave the paper to her so she could continue.

It's clear that the children understand "you break it, you fix it." Before going on to the third kind of logical consequence, time-out, the children have a snack and an outdoor break.

Time-out

When the class comes back in, I return to our discussion. "Time-out is another kind of logical consequence that we'll use in our class. It's used to help students get back in control when they are just beginning to lose self-control," I say. "The teacher tells the student to leave the area where they are having trouble and to spend a little time alone so they can regain control. How many of you have ever heard of this idea?" Most hands go up.

Because some students may have seen time-out used as a punishment or have had other negative experiences with it, I make a point of saying right off the bat exactly what time-out will be in this classroom. "Time-out can mean many different things to different people," I say. "Here's what it means to me. It means someone has made a mistake or broken a rule and needs to regain control. And, because everyone makes mistakes, everyone could spend time in time-out."

I say this matter-of-factly. Still, there are some astonished looks. The children are not used to the idea that time-out is for everyone. I pause to let that concept sink in.

Then I continue. "Time-out is not a punishment. It's a way that teachers help students learn to be responsible and in control of themselves. And finally, time-out happens quickly. You stay in time-out just as long as it takes for you to get back into control, then you come back."

I've given children a lot to take in. Now I want to hear some ideas from them.

"What are some situations when time-out could be helpful?" I ask.

"When we are not listening and just doing what we want to?" one student suggests. Another says, "When we're not letting others get their work done."

"Last year, my teacher put herself in the break chair when she got mad at us!" Joshua exclaims.

"It sounds like she was trying to get her self-control back," I respond. I'm glad for this opportunity to reinforce the idea that anyone, even the teacher, might need a time-out sometimes, and it's not a big deal.

Joshua's remark also provided a nice bridge to the question of what to call time-out, which often goes by different names in different classrooms.

"In Joshua's class last year, the time-out place was called the 'break chair' because that's where you went to take a break and get in control again," I say. "What should we call it in this room this year?"

After a brief discussion, the children decide they'd also like to call it the "break chair." I then tell them that "take a break" will be the words I use to let them know that they need to go to the break chair.

I don't always invite children to help decide what to call time-out. Some years I come up with a name myself, and often I simply call it "time-out." But I try to be alert to clues that the term "time-out" might have particularly negative connotations for that group of students and families. If there are any indications, I choose a different term.

Modeling time-out

We now move to the crucial step of learning how to regain control while in time-out. I use interactive modeling for this lesson. "When you use the break chair, it's important to get back in control as quickly as possible so that you can join the class again," I begin. "I'll model this for you."

Chris has agreed ahead of time to be the "teacher" in this modeling while I play the part of the student. "Let's pretend that I start talking while someone is sharing," I tell the class. "Chris will give me the cue to go to the break chair. Everyone else, watch me during the whole time that I go to the break chair and the whole time I'm in it. Ready, Chris?"

Chris nods. I lean over to whisper to a student sitting next to me.

"Ms. Brady, take a break," Chris says in a steady voice.

I rise slowly and, with a soft sigh, walk to the break chair, which is near our quiet reading area. I sit and stare ahead for about a minute, then move back to my original seat in the circle without a sound.

"What did you notice?" I ask the class.

"You got up and went to the chair when Chris told you to."

"You didn't, like, run, or stomp your feet."

"That's right. What did I do?"

"You walked."

"What did you notice about when I was sitting in the chair?"

The children name several details: I was quiet, not talking to anyone or trying to catch anyone's eye. Just before I came back I looked serious, like I was ready to be back with the group. And I decided when to come back.

I tell the children that when they go to the break chair, they will be deciding when they're ready to come back. But if I see them coming back too early, before they've gotten their control back, or spending too much time in the break chair, then I'll tell them when to come back the next time.

Next I ask the children to think about what exactly a person should be doing while in the break chair. Someone suggests stretching and taking deep breaths, an idea that the others seem to like a lot.

As a final piece of this reflection on time-out, I ask the children to think about how they can be helpful when someone else needs to go to the break chair and regain control.

"We could kinda like ignore them," Chris says.

"How would that help?"

"If I had to go to the break chair, I wouldn't want anyone saying anything to me or looking at me," Chris explains.

"One of our class rules is 'Respect and take care of everybody'," I say. "Leaving someone alone when they are in the break chair is a way of taking care of them."

I conclude the discussion by reminding the students that everyone might need to use the break chair sometimes during the school year, and that's okay.

Explaining Logical Consequences to Families

It's just as important to explain your use of logical consequences to children's families as to the children themselves. Like the children, some families may assume that logical consequences are the same as punishments.

Early in the year, send a letter to families telling them the classroom rules and how they were created. Then briefly describe the three types of logical consequences. To show how logical consequences are different from punishment, you may want to give some examples of their use. Explain that you know children cannot be expected to follow every rule all the time, but that you will be teaching them the importance of the rules. Finally, invite families to ask questions. Following is a sample letter.

Dear Families,

During these first weeks of school, we've been creating our classroom rules and practicing putting them into action. These are rules that we all agree will help everyone in our class make his or her goal for the year come true. Our rules are:

- Respect and take care of everybody.

- Use materials carefully.

- Let everybody learn.

I recognize that no one can be expected to follow the rules 100% of the time. When children make mistakes in following the rules, I'll use "logical consquences" to help them get back on track. Logical consequences are not punishments. They are ways to help children see the effects of their actions and learn self-control and social responsibility.

There are three basic kinds of logical consequences:

Take a break—If a child is losing self-control, the child goes to a designated spot in the room to cool off. The break is short. The child comes back as soon as she or he has regained control. Children may go voluntarily to "take a break."

Loss of privilege—If a child misuses a material or misbehaves during an activity, the child will be told to stop using the material or doing the activity for a short period of time. The privilege will be restored when the child and teacher have talked about how to prevent a similar problem in the future.

"You break it, you fix it"—If a child damages something, the child will be responsible for helping to fix the damage.

My goal is to help children create a caring learning community and develop the skills necessary to be positive members of this community. Learning to live by the rules they've created is an important step. Please let me know if you have any questions.

Sincerely,

Logical Consequences in Action

Below are examples of applications of the three types of logical consequences, along with some things to notice about each scenario. These examples are not meant to be prescriptive, since applying logical consequences is anything but cut-and-dried. There are a number of possible ways to handle every situation. The appropriate response depends on the child's age and temperament, the needs of the rest of the group, the teacher's style, the overall school climate, and other factors.

In deciding how to handle a situation, I try to be clear on what happened and what rule was broken. Some things I consider are whether the behavior is typical developmentally for children that age, whether the child understands the expectations, and what exactly I'm trying to achieve in resolving the situation. All these will affect which type of consequence might be most appropriate and how best to talk to the child.

In many cases, I find that a strategy other than logical consequences is needed. Perhaps I need to go back and role-play something that we didn't role-play before. Perhaps another type of problem-solving strategy such as a class meeting or an individual social conference with the student is called for. (See Appendix A or the book *Solving Thorny Behavior Problems* by Caltha Crowe for more about these problem-solving strategies.) The key is to consider the nuances of each situation and be flexible.

Time-out: Whispering during someone's sharing

The class is gathered in a circle listening to Sara share about a piece of work. Marla starts whispering to her neighbor. "Marla, take a break," the teacher says in an even voice.

Things to notice:

TIME-OUT WAS USED FOR A SMALL THING.

The teacher set a high standard for behavior in this classroom, and she held students to it. Whispering may seem like a small matter, but it's disruptive to Sara and the group. The teacher had worked hard to impress upon students that respecting the learning time of all class members means not whispering or holding side conversations during a student's sharing. Now she was showing that she meant what she said.

THE TEACHER USED A CALM VOICE AND EXPRESSION.

Her demeanor helped students believe that she didn't dislike them, only their behavior.

THE TEACHER TOLD, RATHER THAN ASKED, THE STUDENT TO GO TO TIME-OUT.

I often hear teachers say, "Can you go to time-out now?" or even "Do you need to go to time-out?" Asking children if they need a logical consequence can be confusing at best and an idle threat at worst. It gives the message that the teacher is not in charge. A classroom would quickly become permissive and chaotic if the students were in charge of deciding on their own logical consequences.

Loss of privilege: Disruptive behavior

Jeremy, a fleet-of-foot fourth grader, is the class courier for the week. His job is to deliver the attendance sheet and lunch count to the office each day. On Monday morning, before Jeremy sets off on his errand, his teacher reviews with him the expectations for the job. She sees that Jeremy understands he needs to walk quietly and leave students alone when he walks past classroom doors, even if he sees his friends inside. Monday goes swimmingly. Four or five minutes after the teacher sent Jeremy off with the attendance and lunch sheet, the child returns without incident.

On Tuesday, Jeremy again returns in four or five minutes. But in the teachers' lunchroom later, some teachers report that Jeremy waved hello to students as he walked past classroom doors and that he ran through the cafeteria. After lunch, Jeremy's teacher pulls him aside as the class files in from recess.

"Jeremy, some of the other teachers told me you were waving to your friends and running in the cafeteria when you were doing your errand this morning," the teacher says.

Surprised, Jeremy immediately becomes defensive. "I was just waving a little, and they waved first, and no one was in the cafeteria . . ."

Seeing that Jeremy was making excuses, the teacher stops this thread of talk. "The courier is an important job in this class. But since you didn't handle this responsibility the way that we talked about yesterday morning, I'm going to reassign the job to someone else for Wednesday and Thursday."

Jeremy starts to cry, but the teacher continues calmly: "During those two days I would like you to come up with a plan for how you will do this job responsibly on Friday. We'll talk more about this tomorrow morning. If you need to splash water on your face, you have two minutes before we begin writer's workshop."

As Jeremy goes off to the bathroom, the teacher reflects that given Jeremy's nature, she might have helped him stay in control if she had given him a reminder today before he left for his errand, just as she had done the day before. She makes a mental note to ask Jeremy whether he thinks a reminder Friday morning would help. It wouldn't have to be a verbal reminder. Maybe a sticker to put on his hand that means "Remember our rules." Or perhaps a secret signal she would give him just as he's leaving that means the same thing.

Soon Jeremy returns, looking calmer, and the class begins the writer's workshop.

Things to notice:

FORGETFULNESS OR IMPULSIVENESS WAS NOT ACCEPTED AS AN EXCUSE.

While having empathy for Jeremy's struggles with self-control, the teacher nonetheless held him to the same high standards as the rest of the class. Instead of lowering the standards for Jeremy, the teacher gave him another chance to succeed.

THE TEACHER LOOKED FOR SPECIFIC STRATEGIES TO HELP THE CHILD.

Holding a child to high standards does not mean refusing to help the child meet them. In this case, the teacher was ready to give Jeremy whatever help he needed, be it a secret signal, a sticker, or a verbal reminder.

PRIVILEGE IS RESTORED AFTER A REASONABLE PERIOD OF TIME.

When a privilege is removed for too long, children are more likely to feel they're being punished. They may become angry and stop trusting that their teacher will be fair, or they may feel ashamed and lose faith in their own ability to do the right thing.

When Does a Consequence Become a Punishment?

It can be hard sometimes to know whether a consequence has crossed the line into punishment. Even when a consequence is relevant to the mistake and the teacher communicates with the child about it with respect, it can fail the "realistic" test. "For years I thought I was using logical consequences with my students, especially around writing on desks," one teacher says. "I'd have the children come after school or stay in from recess to wash all of the desks. Obviously this wasn't reasonable. It's like the kid who's attached to the custodian's hip for weeks for writing on the bathroom wall."

I have a personal self-check that I use to see if my responses to children's misbehavior are reasonable. If I catch myself thinking, "I'll make sure you NEVER do this again," I know that I'm being ruled by anger and that I'm headed toward a punishment rather than a logical consequence. At those times I know I need to calm down before deciding on a course of action.

"You break it, you fix it": Putting off cleanup

Max and Danielle are using tempera paints for a social studies project in a corner of the room. At the end of the social studies block, the teacher rings the chime, indicating it's time to clean up.

Later, after the class has left for lunch, the teacher notices that the back corner where Max and Danielle were working is a mess. The paints and other materials have been left out and there is some paint on the floor. He's sorry he didn't see this while the students were in the room but addresses the situation immediately when the class returns.

"Max and Danielle," the teacher says, "after you went to lunch, I noticed the mess in the back corner with the paints." The students grimace.

"I told you we should clean up," Max says to Danielle under his breath.

Danielle begins to explain: "We just had a little more to finish when you rang the chime, so we didn't want to stop. We were going to clean it up later."

"Clean it up now," the teacher says. "Math is about to begin. Let me know when you're done so I can check this area." He then gets the class started on their math work.

A few minutes later, Danielle and Max tell the teacher they've finished cleaning up. Looking over the area, he sees they've done a good job. "This area looks great. You obviously know how to clean up, and I know you understand why it's important that you clean up when I give the signal," he says. "I expect you to do it independently from now on." Max and Danielle then join the class in math.

Things to notice:

"WE WERE PLANNING TO CLEAN UP LATER" ISN'T GOOD ENOUGH.

If the teacher had let this slide, the message would have been that individual agendas are acceptable. In this case, however, they aren't acceptable because there are important reasons for cleaning up at the designated time.

THE TEACHER'S RESPONSE WAS NOT OVERLY HARSH.

Because this was the first time Danielle and Max failed to clean up when they were supposed to, the teacher allowed that it was a simple mistake. He decided that having them clean up the area as soon as possible and clearly stating his expectation for the future were enough. He made a mental note, however, that if the students' behavior becomes a pattern, he might say they can't use the paints until they've shown that they can clean up responsibly. Or he might require them to check in with him after all cleanups for a week, so that he can make sure their areas are tidied up before they start the next activity.

Reflections on Rules at the End of the Year

Periodically throughout the year, I reflect with students on how we're doing in paying attention to our rules—what we're doing well, what we could do better, and what would help us do better. Then, just before school gets out for the year, we do one final reflection. Which rules helped us meet our goals? Which rule was the hardest to follow? Which rule did we like the most? How and why did these rules help us?

Just like I begin the goal-setting process in August by articulating my own goal, in June I think back on the year before asking children to do the same.

The first year I did this review, I sat in the room one afternoon two weeks before school got out and reread our "hopes and dreams" display. I was amazed. Every child had achieved his or her goal, whether it was academic or social. My worries about Joshua, the child who set a social goal for himself, were unfounded. Not only did he make friends, but he achieved significant academic growth as well.

Here's what Joshua himself said at the end of the year: "This year I made two good friends. 'Respect and take care of everybody' is the rule that helped me the most 'cause it helped me learn how to be a good friend."

His classmate Shanice said, "I think 'Use materials carefully' was my favorite rule because we got to learn a lot of stuff like making a short movie on the computer, and we couldn't have done the movies if people weren't safe with the camera and computers."

And finally, Marta said, "My favorite rule was the same as Joshua's. People are nice to each other in this class, and it is a nice place to be."

Creating a nice place to be. There is perhaps no more important reason to have rules in school.

WORK CITED

Crowe, Caltha. (2009). *Solving Thorny Behavior Problems: How Teachers and Students Can Work Together.* Turners Falls, MA: Northeast Foundation for Children, Inc.

Grades 6–8

Middle school is a tumultuous time for children. Not only are their bodies going through enormous physical changes, but how they think, what they think about, and how they relate to others and the world are all changing as well. Uppermost on the minds of these students are questions such as: Who am I? Why am I here? Where do I belong? What's happening to my body? Is this normal? How do I compare to others? Are we going to be graded on this? Who cares? Who says so?

These questions speak clearly of the struggles of young adolescents as they begin to form an identity separate from the adults in their lives and find a path of their own into adulthood. They also reveal a fascinating world of contradictions. On the one hand, being different from adults seems to be the goal of adolescents, and rebelling against authority the preferred strategy. On the other hand, some of the top concerns of adolescents show a vulnerability that betrays a desire for meaningful interactions with adults and authority.

When one thinks about the rebellious side of adolescents, it may seem hopeless for middle school teachers to try to engage students in any activity having to do with school rules. Recently I saw a student in a middle school classroom wearing a black T-shirt bearing a quotation from the wrestling group New World Order. In big block letters the shirt said "Rules and bones are meant to be broken."

But the fact that adolescents also hunger for meaning convinces me that middle school is actually an ideal time to address school rules. The key, of course, lies in where the rules come from. Rules created by adults, sanctioned by other adults, and then handed down to students will immediately become the target of contempt. But rules that middle schoolers develop themselves with caring and respectful guidance from adults often are genuinely respected, even treasured.

The rule-creation process described in this book works well with adolescents because it invites them to use their maturing ability to think abstractly and globally. It also requires students to share and listen to each other's ideas, which taps into adolescents' great interest in the opinions of their peers.

Special Considerations in Creating Rules in Middle School

Two questions frequently come up around using the rules approach described in this book with middle schoolers. One has to do with logistics, the other with adolescents' preoccupation with being "cool."

Logistics

In the typical middle school, where students move through five to seven periods with different teachers in the course of the day, how can teachers structure the rule-creation process so that it's workable and meaningful? There are three possible ways:

Create rules in homeroom or advisory that are then used to make schoolwide rules

This method can work if there is support from the administration, staff, and teachers for a unified schoolwide approach to discipline. Each teacher creates rules with students in homeroom or advisory using the process described in this book. Student representatives from each homeroom/.advisory then gather the rules from all the homerooms/advisories and, with adult guidance, consolidate these rules into three to five all-school rules. These then become the rules that guide the behavior of all students, whether they are in classes, at lunch, in the halls, at their lockers, on the sports field, or on school trips.

Create rules in homeroom or advisory that are then used to make team rules

Many middle schools use a structure in which teachers form teams. Each student in the school is placed with a team and has homeroom or advisory and attends classes with teachers who are part of that team. In this structure, teachers can create a set of rules with their homeroom/advisory students. Student representatives from each homeroom/advisory then gather the rules from all the homerooms/advisories in the team and consolidate them into three to five rules. These become the rules that all students in the team are expected to live by throughout the day.

Create rules in each period of the day

In schools that have neither a team structure nor a schoolwide commitment to a unified discipline policy, teachers can still use the rules approach described in this book. In that scenario, they would go through the rule-creation process with each class, asking students what their goals are for that class—for example, "What is your most important goal for language arts this year?" or "What's your top goal in math this year?" From these goals, each class would produce a set of rules for that class. In language arts, students would be expected to live by the rules they created in language arts; in math they would be expected to live by the rules they created in math; and so forth.

Some teachers go one step further to post the rules from all their classes, then ask students to notice similarities and differences in wording. Talking about these nuances can bring students to a deeper understanding of what the rules really mean.

Of these three methods, having schoolwide or team rules is preferable because these options ensure the greatest continuity of expectations and the least confusion as students move from classroom to classroom. However, even with a separate set of rules in each class period, the message is clear: "In this school, we have high expectations for conduct, and we have faith that you can meet those high expectations."

Adolescent "cool"

During the middle school years, children become more self-conscious, more consumed with questions about identity, and often more defensive. For this reason, it's especially important that teachers in these grades establish a climate of trust in the classroom before asking students to share their goals.

One of the most effective ways of building this trust that I've seen is to begin each day, or most days, with a routine called Circle of Power and Respect, or CPR for short. CPR is the middle school version of Morning Meeting. As in Morning Meeting at the elementary school level, in CPR the whole class gathers in a circle to greet each other, share news or other interesting information, do a group activity, and hear announcements about the day ahead.

CPR offers middle school students stability during a time in their life dominated by tumultuous change. Seated in a circle, all students are seen and acknowledged. Students learn to greet each other with respect, com-

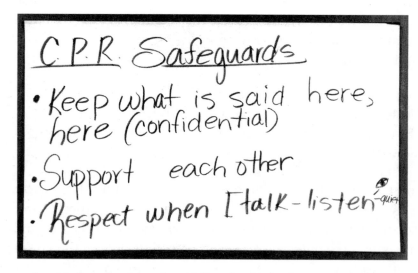

An eighth grade advisory's guidelines for Circle of Power and Respect (CPR), the middle school version of Morning Meeting

municate with power and authority without putting each other down, and listen to one another's stories, triumphs, and fears. As one teacher put it, "In the dog-eat-dog world that many kids live in, CPR offers them another way to be." With CPR to establish a tone of respect and caring, students are more likely to feel safe sharing their goals. (For more about CPR, please see *The Morning Meeting Book* by Roxann Kriete.)

Another important way of building trust is to establish clear classroom routines early on. This includes agreeing on signals for quiet, procedures for entering and leaving the room, and rules for meetings. While one might think that by middle school, students would know the expectations for these basic classroom and social interactions, I've found it best not to make any assumptions. Teaching these routines explicitly is critical for students who don't know them, a good review for those who do, and a clear message to all that in this classroom, calm, orderliness, and respect will reign. Students will more likely feel confident that when they speak, they'll have a receptive and respectful audience. They'll therefore be more willing to share authentic goals.

Creating the Rules

Naming "one most important goal" with middle schoolers

Beginning the rule-creation process by inviting students to each think about their own most important goal can be very effective with middle schoolers. Students this age tend to be attracted to more in-depth pursuits in areas from science to drama, to debate, to music. They generally like taking on or imagining themselves in adult roles. And they're preoccupied with carving out an identity for themselves. All of these make them very willing on the whole to talk about their goals if they know what they say will be taken seriously.

Middle school teachers should begin the process by reflecting on their own top goal for the class and sharing this goal with students, just as elementary school teachers do. One language arts teacher I work with told her students recently, "I hope all students in this class improve their literacy skills and feel safe taking the risks necessary to learn." She then asked her students to think about their past years in school and some things they'd like to accomplish this year in language arts.

It's important to give students this age plenty of time to think through their goals. For example, a teacher might ask students to write in their journals about this topic one day, and then give them a chance to revise their writing the next day. Some teachers choose to make the articulation of goals a homework assignment. After sharing her own hope for the class this year, the teacher might ask students to answer a series of questions in writing at home:

- One thing I'm proud of having accomplished last year is:

- One thing I would like to have done better last year is:

- One important hope, dream, or goal of mine for this year is:

- One thing I will need from my teacher and my fellow students to help me reach this hope, dream, or goal is:

The next day, students can either share their answers openly or anonymously. If the plan is to have anonymous sharing, it's helpful to tell students ahead of time. Knowing that their names will not be revealed can free students to be more honest and serious in naming a personal learning goal.

Two frequent themes among middle schoolers' goals are to achieve academically so they can have a good future and to do well socially. Following are examples of goals from sixth and eighth grade students.

Sixth graders' goals

I hope to learn short division, get good grades, and make lots of friends.

One thing I want to do is learn more about science and learn about batteries.

I hope to get accepted to Vo-Tech by the end of middle school.

I hope to do math in my head and get straight A's.

I want to get good grades so I can go to a good college.

I hope to make the basketball team and get good grades so I can go to the Art School next year.

I would like to make a lot of friends, learn more in social studies and science, and to make the garden look pretty.

Eighth graders' goals

I hope to be able to keep up with my studies so that I will pass the eighth grade with good grades and move to the high school next year.

My hope for this class is that I will always be able to work to the best of my ability. I hope that I will get A's or B's and that I will have a positive attitude when I walk into this class.

One of my personal goals is to learn to speak Spanish so that I can speak with my grandmother on my own.

I hope to participate in one of the school plays this year, either helping with the costumes or making the sets.

This year I hope to increase my circle of friends. I want to make good decisions around class work and homework so that my grades will improve in all of my subjects.

Helping those who resist

Even when teachers take steps to set a climate of authenticity and trust in the classroom, there may be some students who resist naming a goal. Maybe school has been a struggle in the past, so naming a goal feels risky. For these students, I find that asking them to name a goal for the first month or week of school reduces the risk. Keeping students' goals anonymous also helps.

Some children, perhaps fearing the judgment or laughter of peers, may try to make a joke of the process. "My goal is to have no goals" or "My hope is that we have a half day every day," they might say. In *The First Six Weeks of School*, Paula Denton and Roxann Kriete suggest using a "combination of a light touch and serious intent" to handle these situations: "Though you might well wish for school to turn into a video arcade, William, it isn't likely to happen—not this year at least. But I really want school to be a place where all students find enjoyment and get to work at things that really matter to them. I believe there are things that are within the realm of possibility that you could name, things that we could help come true. Do you want to think some more on your own, or would you like me to make some suggestions?" (Denton and Kriete, 2000, p. 77)

When we hold students to the expectation of naming authentic goals, and assure them that their words will be taken seriously, students usually drop their defenses and actually welcome the chance to share what matters to them in school.

Hopes and dreams
for Room 308—

Erica – My hopes and dreams for homeroom and my math class. Is to pass w/good grades and to enjoy homeroom more.

<u>Chelsea</u> – My hopes and dreams are to pass the 8th grade. I also hope that I will get good grades in math and understand the work.

<u>Ibrahim</u> – My hopes and dreams for math are to understand math and have fun.

<u>Constance</u> – My hopes and dreams for this class is to be everything I can be, and to become to be I want to do good and make good grades.

<u>Mary</u> – My hopes and dreams for this class is to bring all my grades up, and to have a good time learning how to understand more math. To pass in all my homework.

Sarah. My hopes and dreams are to be successful, try my best, have fun, and believe I can do it.

Lynne – My hopes and dreams for this year is to get "NJHS" again this year also to not let anyone distract me in the year

William – My hopes and dreams for this class are to pass and get good grades.

Scott – My hopes and dreams for this class is to get good grades and stay on task the whole year and learn new things in math.

Kiara – My hopes and dreams for math is to understand and get at least a B.

Some eighth graders' hopes and dreams for the school year

Involving Families in Naming Goals

In addition to doing the goal-setting activity with students, many middle school teachers ask the students' families to name their goals for their children. Here's a sample letter that one teacher sends home:

Dear Parents/Guardians,

I have the pleasure of being your child's homeroom teacher. Since the beginning of this school year, teachers and students have been sharing goals and we would like you to be part of the process.

Please take a few minutes to share what you want your child to accomplish during this school year. I have divided the accomplishments into two areas.

1. What academic gains do you wish for your child?

2. What social goals do you have for your child?

Thank you for taking this time to share your goals. I look forward to working together to help your child reach these goals.

Sincerely,

There are great benefits to involving families in this way. It helps establish a sense of community and trust between school and home. Hearing families' goals can be enlightening for the teacher and reassuring when those goals align well with the teacher's, which is often the case. And asking for families' goals shows the students that their teachers and families are working together to help them.

Generating the rules: "What will help you meet your hopes and dreams?"

The next step is to generate rules by discussing what needs to occur in order for class members to meet their goals. Following is an example of how Ms. Katsuren, a seventh grade teacher, guides a discussion about rules in a school that uses a team teaching approach.

"Yesterday we talked about our hopes and dreams for this year," she begins. "Now let's think about what rules we'll need in school if we're going to make those hopes and dreams happen."

Ms. Katsuren asks students to get out some paper and respond to two questions:

1. What is something that other students and teachers could do to help you meet your goal?

2. What is something you can do to try to meet your goal?

After students have written their responses, they pair up to share and clarify their statements.

When all pairs have finished, Ms. Katsuren resumes the discussion. The day before, the students noticed two common themes in their goals—academic goals such as getting good grades or learning more about a subject, and social goals such as making new friends. Ms. Katsuren focuses first on the academic. "Those of you who named an academic goal, what ideas did you come up with for how others can help you?" She has a chart ready for recording students' ideas.

"I get easily interrupted. So I need the other kids to quit bugging me so I can get my work done," one student says.

Wanting to steer students toward positively stated rules (what to do) rather than negatively stated ones (what not to do), Ms. Katsuren says, "If we shouldn't bug you, what should we do to help you?"

"People could let me learn and ask me if they're interrupting me."

**Classroom Rules
201**

Listen.
Respect! Respect!
Be responsible.
Know the school rules
Always give 100%.

Hr. 206 Rules

1. Respect Others.
2. Respect the Classroom and the Materials.
3. Be prepared for Class and try your Best. Jessica
4. Be safe.

8ᵗʰ Grade Class Rules

1. Treat others the way you **want** them and expect them to treat you.
2. Pay attention and talk on your own time
3. Be prepared for class.
4. Respect other's property.
5. Be organized and take care of all materials and our environment.

Rules from sixth, seventh, and eighth grade classrooms

"So does it make sense if I write down 'Let students learn'?" Students nod.

"Now, what can you do to help yourself with your learning?"

The students respond with their ideas. Here's a sampling: "Let others know when they're interrupting me"; "Move to a different place to work"; "I can just tell myself to keep working." Ms. Katsuren writes these ideas on the chart, which now looks like this:

Goal	Rules: How others can help	Rules: How we can help ourselves
Academic Goal	Let students learn. Ask if they are interrupting.	Let others know when they are interrupting. Find a better place to work. Tell ourselves to keep working.
Social Goal		
Other		

Continuing in this way, the group generates more ideas for rules in the "Academic" category, then does the same for the "Social" category, and finally for the "Other" category, which includes goals related to sports, music, and other pursuits that don't fall in either the academic or social arenas. By the end of the exercise, the students have a long list of rules that are clearly and positively stated. And, Ms. Katsuren believes, they see more clearly that they have a responsibility to themselves and others in this community.

A few good final rules

During the next two advisories, the group synthesizes the long list of rules into a few broad ones that encompass all the specific ideas. Generally students' rules fall into the categories of respect for self, respect for others, respect for the learning environment, and respect for school materials and property. This class is no different. After noting similarities among their specific ideas and playing with wording, the students come up with the following as their advisory rules:

- Treat everyone with respect.

- Allow everyone to learn at his/her own pace.

- Help to create a safe and caring environment.

- Accept individuals for who they are.

All the teachers on Ms. Katsuren's team are committed to this approach to rule creation and have agreed ahead of time to consolidate the individual advisory rules into one final set for the team. This will ensure that expectations are consistent from classroom to classroom. To do this, each advisory elects two students to serve on a committee.

Over the next few days, the committee, guided by one of the teachers on the team, sorts through the rules from all the advisories, looking for overlaps, combining similar ideas, and discussing wording that would best capture the spirit behind the original rules. The result is a set of three easy-to-remember rules that encompass all the ideas from the advisories and that can help all students on the team realize their hopes and dreams (see box on right).

Team 7 Rules

1. Treat everyone with respect.

2. Let each person learn in his/her own way.

3. Keep our community safe and clean.

When the committee members report back, each advisory makes a poster of the team rules and puts it up on a wall near an exhibit of the group's hopes and dreams. Throughout the year, the display will be a reminder to students of the high standards for conduct at school and the purpose behind these standards.

Supporting the Rules with Teacher Language

For the rest of the year, but especially over the next few weeks, it's important to talk with students about what their team rules might look like when applied to the everyday life of school. A critical part of the talking is for the teacher to simply acknowledge examples of positive behavior that he notices.

I saw a simple but effective instance of this recently at a middle school I work in:

It was several weeks into the school year. Alexi, a new student, had just walked into homeroom. The teacher introduced Alexi to the class before Circle of Power and Respect (CPR). Then, without prompting from the teacher, the class chose a CPR greeting that would help Alexi learn names. During the activity portion of the meeting, one student offered to partner up with Alexi so she might be more comfortable.

The next day, the teacher told the group what he noticed. "Yesterday when Alexi came in, many of you made an effort to welcome and take care of her and you chose a greeting that would allow her to learn names. Does anyone have a suggestion for a greeting or activity today that will continue what we started yesterday?" By naming the positive behavior he saw, the teacher reinforces its importance.

"We could do the Adjective greeting and then check to see how many we all remember," one student suggests. Students explain the steps to Alexi, and the greeting takes off around the circle.

Notice that the teacher didn't praise the students. He didn't say "you were so good yesterday" or "I'm so proud of you" or even "good job," statements that make a value judgment about the students. Instead, he acknowledged their actions: He named the specific behavior that he noticed and matter-of-factly asked how students might do more of the same.

Many teachers, after trying this kind of language, find that students are more likely to continue to be kind and responsible. Praise isn't necessary. In fact, middle school students seem to dislike praise, even in private. In front of the whole class, praise has the effect of setting them apart as a "teacher's favorite." A simple acknowledgment, on the other hand, serves as a reflection of their competence.

Besides using reinforcing language, Alexi's teacher uses two other language techniques to support rules. The first is reminding language, which he uses before starting an activity, to set students up to succeed. "Who can remind the class about how to handle the microscopes?" He also uses reminders when students begin to act inappropriately so that they have a chance to pull themselves back on track. "Jeremiah, remember what we said about giving everyone a chance to speak?"

And when students continue to misbehave, this teacher uses clear redirecting language to tell the student to stop and to change course. When Daniel flings a book carelessly onto the floor after using it, the teacher says, "Daniel, our rule says that we will take care of our materials. That book belongs on the shelf."

In addition to using language to support positive behavior, middle school teachers can also use interactive modeling and role-playing. With appropriate adjustments in the language used and in the situations modeled and role-played, these strategies can be as effective in middle school as in elementary school. (See Chapter Two for information about interactive modeling and role-playing.)

Teaching Logical Consequences

Having students formulate goals, working with them to create rules, and using effective teacher language are all discipline strategies that lay the groundwork for responsible decision-making among students. These strategies increase the likelihood that students will make positive behavior choices. It would be naive, however, to hope that they will completely prevent misbehavior.

It's not that middle schoolers will break rules because they are middle schoolers. It's that middle schoolers will break rules because they are human beings. Students break rules for the same reasons that adults, including their teachers and the school staff, break rules.

At a recent staff meeting at one middle school, the principal reminded the staff to turn in a questionnaire required by the Department of Education. The staff's various explanations and comments about why they hadn't turned in the form sounded remarkably similar to what middle schoolers might say or think when confronted with a school rule.

What staff said	What students say or think
"What survey?"	"What rule?"
"I thought it wasn't due until next week."	"I need to do it now?"
"Oh yeah, I forgot. I'll turn it in later."	"I forgot."
"What did that form look like?"	"What am I supposed to do?"
"You were serious about that?"	"That's a real rule?"
"I hate doing DOE surveys."	"I hate that rule!"

Remembering that at times we all break rules helps teachers have empathy for students who break rules. That empathy is crucial. It's what leads us to remain respectful of the child's dignity and choose reasonable, non-punitive ways of handling the situation.

Make no mistake, however: Empathy should not stop us from holding students accountable for their actions. Always, we need to let students know that the rules are important and must be taken seriously. Our classes will be in chaos if accountability is absent.

Using logical consequences helps ensure this accountability. And it often does something else. It entrusts students with the task of righting a wrong. This trust is deeply important to adolescents. They want to be given the opportunity to show that they can manage their lives in responsible and caring ways. As Chapter Three makes clear, two of the three types of logical consequences—"you break it, you fix it" and loss of privilege—do just that. They show students the effects of their mistakes and provide students a way to correct them. Both the standard of conduct and students' integrity are maintained.

Introducing logical consequences to students

Soon after the rules have been created, teachers can introduce the idea of logical consequences to students. When and how they do this depends in part on whether they teach in a team structure. In schools that have teams, all teachers on a team might agree to dedicate two or three homerooms or advisories in one week to the discussion of logical consequences. The teachers meet on each of these days to share what went well and what points they might need to review or re-emphasize with their students.

Starting the discussion

I start the discussion of logical consequences with students by talking about how it's hard to follow rules sometimes.

"I notice that you've been paying attention to our rules and using them in many situations. I also know that there will be times when we forget the rules or maybe choose not to follow the rules. Which of our team rules is the hardest to follow?"

"Treat others the way you want to be treated," one student says right away.

"Why is that rule hard to follow?"

"Because I don't mind it when kids call me certain names, but they don't like to be treated that way, so I need to remember that, and it's hard."

"Are you talking about street language and neighborhood slang?"

"Yeah, like some kids get mad if I use certain language. I'm not going to give you an example now 'cause I don't want them to get mad all over again. But I like that language."

Back when the students decided to adopt the Golden Rule, we talked about this very issue. I had anticipated that some students might take the rule literally: "If I wouldn't mind being teased about being short, then it's okay for me to tease other people about being short." So I opened a conversation then about what the rule really meant. After a fascinating discussion, the students came to realize that it meant we should treat everyone with respect, just like we all want respect ourselves. But they also learned that part of respecting people is to accept that what feels good or bad to them may be different from what feels good or bad to us.

Not surprisingly, this idea continues to prove challenging, and I'm glad someone is calling attention to it again.

"So if we're going to follow this rule," I say, "we have to learn what offends other people and what doesn't, rather than using ourselves as the standard, and that's hard to do, right?" Heads nod.

"And do you remember some of the ways we said we can learn this?"

"Listen to what people say"; "Just ask them"; "Watch them and see what they laugh about and get upset about," the students say.

Not wanting to sidetrack too long from the original focus of this conversation, I say, "So taking other people's perspectives is important but hard to do. What else can make it hard to follow rules?"

The students give a list including "It's hard to follow them when you're angry" and "You just forget when you're in a hurry."

"One of the ways that a teacher helps students live by the rules is by holding them accountable with logical consequences. How many of you have heard of logical consequences before?" Many hands go up.

Because some parents and other teachers may take a different approach to using consequences, I take out a chart that spells out what I mean by logical consequences so there will be no confusion.

"You can see from this chart that consequences are respectful, relevant, and realistic," I say. "This means that the consequence would somehow be related to the mistake and would be reasonable, and that the discussion about the mistake would be respectful." It's important to assure students of these things early on.

Logical Consequences

How they help us	What they look like	Three kinds
Help us stay connected to the rules	Respectful	"You break it, you fix it"
Help us avoid similar problems in the future	Relevant	Loss of privilege
Keep us and everyone else safe	Realistic	Time-out or break time
Help us learn self-control		

Explaining "you break it, you fix it" and "loss of privilege"

"One of our rules is 'help to create a safe and caring environment.' What's an example of a time when this rule might be broken?"

"The other day, one group didn't put away their trade books and then we had to look for them the next day," Roger says.

"Wasn't that your group, Roger?" Brittany teases.

"Well, yeah, but the rule was broken," Roger says, laughing.

"In that case, looking for the books cut into that group's work time so they couldn't finish the assignment. They had to find a time to make up for that," I say. "How about if someone decides to use a ruler to prop open the window and the ruler gets broken? What might happen then?"

"They would need to replace the ruler. Or maybe fix it, if that's possible," one student answers.

"That's what 'you break it, you fix it' means. You find a way to fix a mistake that you made. Can anyone think of a time when someone lost the use of a material because they didn't use it properly?"

"Last year, some kid went on Facebook in the computer lab and couldn't use the computer lab for a long time," Jeremiah says.

Veronica volunteers, "My brother took the car out after curfew and my parents won't let him have it back until he can show them that he can be trusted."

"In all of your classes this year, not following the rules for the use of a material may mean that you won't get to use the material for a while. That's what loss of privilege means. When you demonstrate you know how to use the materials responsibly and can make good decisions, you'll be able to use the materials again."

Revisiting time-out

I begin the discussion about time-out by asking how many students have heard of it. Almost every hand goes up. One student groans.

"Time-out can mean a lot of different things to different people. Here's what it means to me and the other teachers on this team," I say. "It's when you leave the scene for a while to collect yourself when you're starting to get frustrated or impulsive, and then you come back to the group when you feel you have your self-control back. What are some times when time-out could be helpful?"

"When kids are interrupting during a meeting," Vong responds.

"Or when someone's just messing around with the science equipment and not doing any work," Rachel says.

"Or when someone's mad and starts yelling at other kids," another student adds.

"Well, by now you all know that I believe everyone makes mistakes, including teachers, so I expect that at one time or another, everyone might get to use the time-out area. And going to time-out doesn't mean you're a bad person; it just means you need to leave the group for a while to regain self-control."

Students in middle school generally don't need much more explanation about time-out than this, so I move quickly to enlisting these students' help in setting up the time-out area. "My advisory group last year decided to put up some vacation posters in the time-out area because posters like that have a calming influence. Would you like to keep the same posters or look for your own?" The student who groaned earlier suddenly looks more interested.

After a bit of discussion, the students decide that the following Monday they would bring in posters they think are calming, then vote on which ones to use. We then turn to the question of what to call time-out.

One student says, "Last year we called it 'vacation' and the teacher would tell us that we needed a vacation." The students decide they like that wording. I tell them I'll check with the other teachers on the team to see what other students suggested.

Using interactive modeling to teach time-out

Even with middle school students, it's important to model time-out. Though most will have experienced time-out, it's unlikely they've all experienced the same approach to it. Interactive modeling allows everyone to get on the same page and see afresh what respectful time-out behavior looks like. It also helps remove the stigma of time-out.

For this modeling session, I set up a scenario in which a student is sharing about an assignment, and another begins carrying on a side conversation with a neighbor. Interestingly, most middle school students get into interactive modeling, and this group is no different. One student readily volunteers to play the sharer, another the teacher, and I play the part of the interrupter.

The modeling begins. The "sharer" starts, "The reason I chose this book for my report . . ."

"Psst, psst, psst," I whisper to a neighbor.

"Ms. Brady, take a vacation," the "teacher" says.

Doing my best imitation of a twelve-year-old, I get up, walk with a resigned air to the chair, and plunk myself down. I slouch low. I look at my fingernails, chew them. I check the clock, take a deep breath, and sigh quietly. After another forty-five seconds, I return to the circle.

The students have been watching intently, suppressing giggles. Their amusement, however, hasn't kept them from taking in the important details of my behavior. When I ask them what they noticed, they said, "You got up and went to the chair when Sheldon asked you to"; "You didn't make a face at anybody while you were leaving the circle"; "You kept your face, um, solemn"; "You came back on your own. It wasn't the teacher who told you when to come back"; "You were in the vacation chair for less than a minute."

I piggyback on this last observation to make a point about not lingering too long in vacation. "That was all the time that I needed to get back in control. Some students spend two minutes in the vacation chair, but usually people don't spend more than three. It's important to return to work as soon as possible."

Then I ask, "What about everyone else in the room? How should they act when someone has to go to vacation?" It's important for students to realize they all have a role to play in helping the person regain self-control.

"Everyone should continue what they're doing and let that person do what they need to do," one student responds.

"Exactly. Would anyone else like to practice moving to the vacation chair?"

We do one or two more rounds before ending the modeling session.

Responding to Misbehavior

To use logical consequences effectively, teachers need to think about what's appropriate in each situation rather than follow a prescription. This is as true in middle school as it is at lower grade levels. Deciding on an appropriate logical consequence requires getting clear about how best to help this child—with this learning style, this background, this temperament—return to positive behavior.

One way that middle school differs from elementary school, however, is the increased premium that students place on "saving face." Now, more than ever, students need teachers to speak to them privately, to not call attention to them, and to treat them "like adults."

The following are examples of responding to misbehavior at the middle school level. They are not meant to be a recipe, but to show the range of possible ways to respond to misbehavior and to offer some tips for responding effectively.

Showing disrespect to a classmate

It's late November, and Mr. Freid's eighth grade class has been learning about different cultural traditions, beliefs, and rituals. At today's Circle of Power and Respect, students are sharing whether their families observe Thanksgiving and, if so, how they usually do it.

As Melissa explains her family's Thanksgiving rituals, Sarah tsks loudly from across the circle and rolls her eyes. Everyone notices, and Melissa is obviously flustered. "Sarah, take a break," Mr. Freid says. Sarah, looking upset, leaves the area for the time-out spot. Mr. Freid is puzzled by Sarah's behavior because she has never shown disrespect to anyone in the class, and she and Melissa are good friends.

Mr. Freid usually lets students come back from time-out without any discussion. The understanding is that in most cases, students simply need a break from the action and are able to decide on their own when they're ready to come back to the group. No talk is necessary. In this case, however, Mr. Freid senses that he needs to have a conversation with Sarah and possibly with both girls. After a while Sarah returns to the meeting circle.

As the students return to their desks after the meeting, Mr. Freid goes over to Sarah. "Sarah, I need to talk with you about what happened when Melissa was sharing." Sarah crosses her arms and avoids eye contact. "I was surprised by what I saw. I know it's not like you to disrupt meetings," Mr. Freid says. "I hope we can clear this up."

Her eyes filling with tears, Sarah says, "I wasn't trying to cause problems. Melissa and I have just been fighting . . ."

Mr. Freid guides Sarah to a private area of the room and says, "I noticed that you were able to come back to the group and show self-control immediately, so things look good there. The bigger problem seems to be finding a way to talk with Melissa and to make sure that you both come out of this feeling okay. Will you need help with that?"

"Maybe. It's about her new boyfriend."

Knowing that students generally like and trust Ms. Rice, the school social worker, Mr. Freid suggests asking her to mediate in this situation. Sarah agrees to give it a try, and Mr. Freid picks up the wall phone to call Ms. Rice.

Commentary

It was important that Mr. Freid told Sarah to go to time-out even though this was the first time she showed this kind of disrespect. This sends Sarah the message that however understandable her behavior might be, she needs to get herself back in control. Using time-out democratically for anyone who needs it also helps show the class that it's a strategy to help all students, not a punishment for chronic "troublemakers."

Note also that while Mr. Freid was concerned with handling the immediate disruption, he recognized that the bigger problem here was the strained friendship between Sarah and Melissa. In seventh and eighth grade, school life can be full of challenges related to evolving relationships. Mr. Freid sensed that Sarah and Melissa's problem was bigger than what the girls could handle alone and warranted some adult intervention.

He later found out that when Melissa's new boyfriend came into the picture, she increasingly wanted to spend time with him alone, leaving Sarah feeling shunned. Ms. Rice was able to help Melissa and Sarah sort through their feelings and guide them in redefining their friendship.

Misusing a scalpel

During science class, the students are preparing to dissect owl pellets. They've just had a modeling session on how to use the dissection tools, with an emphasis on the scalpel.

The students are trying to reconstruct the remains of the creatures that the owls ate. Working in pairs at lab tables, they transfer bones and other identifiable matter onto pieces of oak tag. Two partners begin to talk about the scalpels.

"Look at how sharp these things are!" Elise exclaims.

"Yeah, it's hard keeping the scalpel steady with these gloves on, too," her partner Roman replies.

"How sharp do you think these are?"

"Sharp enough. Just go slow, like Ms. Cook said."

"Let's see if they can cut the oak tag."

"I wouldn't do that if I were you," Roman says.

"What's it going to hurt?" Elise asks. She picks up the paper and cuts it in a sweeping motion.

Ms. Cook sees her doing this. She walks over to the pair and says quietly, "Elise, stop. Put the scalpel down."

"Told you," Roman says under his breath.

"Roman, put your scalpel down, too, for a minute. Elise, we just talked about using these scalpels for one cutting purpose. Do you remember what we said?"

"That we should only cut the pellets with them. I was just trying to see how sharp my scalpel was."

"Yeah, it's pretty sharp. Do you remember why we said we should only cut the pellets with these?"

" 'Cause cutting other things will dull the blade."

"That's right," Ms. Cook says. "I'll be putting this scalpel away for the rest of the period. We'll talk again before you finish this lab tomorrow. We'll decide then whether you can give the scalpel another try. Right now, look on with Roman as he does some dissecting. You may want to use the magnifying glass to help you identify any bones that he finds."

Commentary

Ms. Cook understood it was probably just innocent curiosity that made Elise momentarily forget or ignore the fact that the scalpels were to be used to cut only one thing. But she also wondered if Elise somehow missed or misunderstood what was covered in the modeling. If it had been a less dangerous tool, Ms. Cook would have given her a reminder and let her continue to use it. But because it was such a sharp instrument and its specific use and care were so critical, she felt it was appropriate to take the tool away immediately.

However, it was important that Ms. Cook assured Elise that they would talk about her regaining the use of the scalpel after one period. This showed her faith in Elise's ability to show more responsibility.

After taking the scalpel away, Ms. Cook directed Elise to look on with Roman and help identify the bones that he found. This was a deliberate move. Shifting the focus away from the student's mistake back to the assignment at hand can help the student save face. Not only that, it underscores the importance of academic work and helps reinforce the idea that the reason to take care of classroom equipment is to allow students to do that work well.

When Ms. Cook and Elise talked the next day, Ms. Cook saw that Elise was indeed unclear on a few of the details of safe and proper scalpel use, so she did some individualized modeling with her before letting her use the tool again. It's not unusual for some students to need such additional modeling.

In this incident, Ms. Cook intervened in time to stop Elise from dulling the scalpel, but if Elise had dulled it enough to make it unusable for this project, Ms. Cook would have talked to her about possible ways to replace the tool or otherwise repair the situation.

Late to class

It's the last week of April in what has been a very warm New England spring. The good weather has added to students' usual restlessness at this time of year, and many are having a hard time making it to class on time. Since school resumed after April break, Ms. Robles has given students extra reminders about their responsibilities. Today, several minutes after she closes the door and begins class, two students walk in.

"Good morning, Derrick and Jackson. Class started eight minutes ago," Ms. Robles says.

Derrick and Jackson look at one another sheepishly. Jackson says, "Yeah, we're late. Sorry. Derrick was showing me something." Ms. Robles notes to herself that this is the second time in three weeks that these two students have been late.

"I'll see you later today to talk about this. Come to this room at 2:30," Ms. Robles says, then continues with class.

At 2:30, the students show up. "Hello, Jackson and Derrick," Ms. Robles says. "We need to talk about your arriving late to class."

Jackson starts to explain. "We left math a couple of minutes late and then lost track of time talking at our lockers. Derrick got a new jacket over April break and was showing it to me."

"That sounds pretty important, but getting to class on time is very important too," Ms. Robles responds.

"We promise it won't happen again."

"Let's make a plan to make sure. What would help you keep track of the time?"

Derrick and Jackson look at each other and shrug. With some prompting from Ms. Robles, however, they soon decide that Derrick could set his watch to beep one minute before class starts. They also decide they could "walk and talk." The two students and the teacher agree to give this plan a try.

Commentary

Ms. Robles understood the students' mood at this time of year, thus the extra reminders about their responsibilities. But she didn't let their restlessness become an excuse for lowering the standards in her classroom. When Derrick and Jackson were late a second time, she realized that reminders alone weren't going to be enough for them, and that a more pointed conversation was needed. She also recognized that this was a situation that called for a firm, clear redirection and some practical problem-solving rather than one of the three basic types of logical consequences.

Skillfully, she delayed the conversation rather than taking class time to have it. By simply telling the students to come back at 2:30, she minimized the disruption to the class while still letting the boys know that their lateness was something that needed to be dealt with squarely.

When the conversation did take place, it was important that Ms. Robles helped Derrick and Jackson make a practical plan for getting to class on time. This helped prevent the conversation from feeling punitive, giving it instead a positive purpose.

Moreover, Ms. Robles let the students take the lead in making the plan, prompting them as needed but not imposing a plan on them. This is especially important in middle school, when children crave being treated like adults and put such a high premium on taking charge of their own lives. Ms. Robles knew that the more input Derrick and Jackson had in creating the plan, the more invested they'd be in making it work.

A clique excludes a classmate

The students in Ms. Smythe's social studies class are beginning a project on landforms. Ms. Smythe has asked students to form groups of three or four and decide how to divide up the tasks required for this period's assignment. Two friends, Shawna and Nalee, quickly grab Maika to form a group.

When a fourth girl, Roslyn, asks to join them, the three say they have enough people in their group already. Roslyn walks back to her desk and sits down. Seeing Roslyn sitting alone, Ms. Smythe goes over and asks if she has found a group to work with yet.

"I asked Shawna and Nalee if I could work with them, and they said they have enough," Roslyn says. Ms. Smythe sees right away that Roslyn is having a hard time bouncing back from the rebuff and needs some prodding to find another work group.

Glancing over at the girls, who are looking Roslyn's way, Ms. Smythe says, "I notice that Tony and José have asked Angelica to work with them. Would you like to ask to join their group?"

Roslyn approaches Tony, José, and Angelica and is welcomed into their group. Ms. Smythe waits to make sure that Roslyn is set, then walks over to Shawna, Nalee, and Maika. "I understand you turned someone away from working with you. Remember I said each group can have up to four people?" she says to them.

"We knew that, but we didn't want to work with Roslyn," Nalee says. "We don't want to hang around with her. She's not one of our friends."

"This project is not a social event," Ms. Smythe responds. "It's about working together to do our best learning, which is one of our class rules. You can work in a cooperative way with people who aren't your friends. When we change work groups next week, the three of you will need to split up. We'll talk specifically about your choices next Monday. Right now you may take out your rubric and start choosing tasks."

Commentary

Learning can be a tricky business at the middle school level, when children's social affairs loom large. Students need to have choices around their learning, but as Ms. Smythe demonstrates, when the social agenda interferes with working and learning together productively, the teacher needs to remind students of the purpose of working together.

Academic learning aside, adolescents need to learn that excluding someone, and clique behavior in general, is hurtful and unacceptable socially. Ms. Smythe made that point when she told the girls to split up the following week. Note that she didn't lecture; she simply told them they'd have to find new workmates. When it comes to logical consequences, the less said in general, the better. It's best to let the consequence do the job.

Note also that Ms. Smythe didn't split up the girls right away or make them take Roslyn into their group. Forcing students to work together when all parties are aware of the rejection can be uncomfortable and can backfire. Instead she gave them the opportunity to form their own inclusive groups the following Monday, when work groups are scheduled to change. That way, it's less likely anyone will feel embarrassed or shamed. And before instructing students to change groups on Monday, Ms. Smythe will talk with the whole class about the importance of being inclusive and working with a variety of classmates.

The Power of Many

When an individual teacher uses the approach to discipline described in this book, the classroom can take on a whole different tone. But when a team of teachers or, better yet, a whole school uses the approach, the effect can be even more powerful.

Having a comprehensive schoolwide discipline plan is perhaps particularly important in middle school. When teachers see any given group of students for only a period a day, they have to rely more on a larger environment that supports the discipline approach they use during their time with the students.

I've seen again and again what a difference it can make when all teachers and staff at a school use the same approach to discipline. I remember a sixth grade girl who struggled with self-esteem, had many social problems, and was constantly in trouble. In fact, she seemed to crave the attention she got from acting out, and her antics were often designed to get herself caught. The more witnesses to the crime and punishment, the better.

Her biggest thrill, however, seemed to come from getting lots of other students to go along with her so they would all get in trouble together. This went well for a while until the adults in the school began moving from an autocratic discipline approach to the approach described in this book. Within a year, the changes in the school climate were noticeable. Students were more invested in making positive behavior choices, relationships between adults and students were less adversarial, and communications among students became healthier and more respectful.

By year two, the improvements were even more dramatic. During that year, this child left to attend another school. The following year when she returned, she sensed that something had changed. One day early in the school year, the student was sent to the principal's office alone for cutting class.

When the principal asked her why she was cutting class, she looked at him with complete exasperation, threw up her arms, and asked, "What are you doing to the kids in this school? This school is whacked! A few years ago I could have found ten kids to get in trouble with me. Now I can't even find one!"

WORKS CITED

Denton, Paula, and Kriete, Roxann. (2000). *The First Six Weeks of School.* Greenfield, MA: Northeast Foundation for Children, Inc.

Kriete, Roxann (with Lynn Bechtel). (2002). *The Morning Meeting Book.* Greenfield, MA: Northeast Foundation for Children, Inc.

Collaborative Problem-Solving Strategies

Geoff consistently acts out during math practice time. His teacher has tried using reminders and redirections, sending him to take-a-break, and having him sit in a seat away from his buddies and close to the teacher, but nothing seems to be working. In other parts of classroom life Geoff is successful and cheerful, but it seems as though math throws some kind of misbehavior switch in him. His teacher decides to have a problem-solving conference with Geoff to see if they can figure out together how to make math a more successful experience.

———————————————

Mrs. Jennings's fifth grade class has been squabbling a lot during outdoor recess. Mrs. Jennings suspects that changes in recess scheduling might be part of the problem. Her students are accustomed to having the playground equipment to themselves but now have to share the equipment with several other classes. She's constantly using reminders and redirections; she has revisited routines for safe use of the climbing equipment and reviewed how to apply the class rules to life on the playground, but still the bickering continues. She decides to hold a class meeting to discuss the issue.

———————————————

Jenna and April were assigned to work together on a social studies project but are having a difficult time figuring out how to share materials and work space. Jenna tends to be neat and precise; April is messier. Their teacher thinks that their strengths will complement each other but the reality is that the two girls spend a lot of time feeling irritated with each other. The low-level irritation boils over when April spills water on a poster that Jenna had filled with careful printing. Their teacher considers assigning them to different partners but thinks that there is value to their learning to work together, so she guides them through a student-to-student conflict resolution process.

Collaborative problem-solving can take a variety of forms depending on the students involved and the nature of the problems. Following are brief descriptions of three kinds of collaborative problem-solving, along with resources for learning more.

Teacher-Student Problem-Solving Conference

This is a structured conference carefully planned by the teacher. The conference focuses on one problem area. The teacher begins by noticing strengths that the student brings to the classroom, then describes the problem she's noticed. Together, the child and teacher speculate about why this behavior is happening and come up with potential solutions. The conference ends with an agreement to try one of the solutions, with a time specified for the teacher and student to talk about how things are going.

Class Meetings

Class meetings use a structured format to talk about and resolve issues that affect the entire class. Class meetings can be held as needed or on a regular schedule. Teachers might hold class meetings preventively, before a potentially problematic situation, or reactively, in response to a problem situation. Before holding class meetings, it's important to establish meeting rules and to teach and practice procedures for talking and listening that will help all children feel safe.

Student-to-Student Conflict Resolution

This is a highly structured interaction between two students that allows each student to state his or her point of view and be listened to respectfully. The goal of the interaction is to reach a mutual understanding of the situation and an agreement about how to resolve the problem. Teachers will want to carefully teach all of the procedures needed for successful conflict resolution: how to ask a classmate for a conflict resolution meeting, how to use "I-messages," how to listen respectfully, how to respond, and how to conclude the conversation. While children are learning these skills, teachers will want to supervise the conversations.

Problem-Solving Strategies:
Responsive Classroom Resources

"Coaching Children in Handling Everyday Conflicts" by Caltha Crowe. *Responsive Classroom Newsletter*, Vol. 21, No. 1, February 2009. Online: www.responsiveclassroom.org.

Sammy and His Behavior Problems: Stories and Strategies from a Teacher's Year by Caltha Crowe. Northeast Foundation for Children, Inc., 2010.

Solving Thorny Behavior Problems: How Teachers and Students Can Work Together by Caltha Crowe. Northeast Foundation for Children, Inc., 2009.

"Teacher-Child Problem-Solving Conferences: Involving Children in Finding Solutions to Their Behavior Problems" by Ruth Sidney Charney. *Responsive Classroom Newsletter*, Vol. 16, No. 4, Fall 2004. Online: www.responsiveclassroom.org.

"A Teacher Shares: Erica's Surprising Insight" by Caltha Crowe. *Responsive Classroom Newsletter*, Vol. 22, No. 1, February 2010. Online: www.responsiveclassroom.org.

Teaching Children to Care: Classroom Management for Ethical and Academic Growth, K–8 by Ruth Sidney Charney. Northeast Foundation for Children, Inc., 2002.

Recommended Resources

Theory

Democracy and Education by John Dewey. The Free Press, 1997 (originally published in 1916).

Discipline Without Tears: How to Reduce Conflict and Establish Cooperation in the Classroom, revised edition, by Rudolf Dreikurs, Pearl Cassel, and Eva Dreikurs Ferguson. Wiley, 2004.

Educating Moral People: A Caring Alternative to Character Education by Nel Noddings. Teachers College Press, 2002.

Emotional Intelligence: Why It Can Matter More Than IQ, 10th anniversary edition, by Daniel Goleman. Bantam, 2006.

Maintaining Sanity in the Classroom: Classroom Management Techniques, 2nd edition, by Rudolf Dreikurs, Bernice Grunwald, and Floy Pepper. Taylor & Francis, Inc., 1998.

The Moral Child: Nurturing Children's Natural Moral Growth by William Damon. The Free Press, 1990.

The Moral Intelligence of Children: How to Raise a Moral Child by Robert Coles. Plume, 1998.

Nurture Shock: New Thinking About Children by Po Bronson and Ashley Merryman. Twelve, 2009.

The Philosophy of Moral Development: Moral Stages and the Idea of Justice by Lawrence Kohlberg. Harper & Row, 1981.

The Quality School: Managing Students Without Coercion by William Glasser. HarperPerennial, 1998.

Teacher and Child: A Book for Parents and Teachers by Haim Ginott. Avon Books, 1975.

Practice

Building Emotional Intelligence: Techniques to Cultivate Inner Strength in Children by Linda Lantieri and Daniel Goleman. Sounds True, Inc., 2008.

The Caring Teacher's Guide to Discipline: Helping Students Learn Self-Control, Responsibility, and Respect by Marilyn Gootman. Corwin Press, 2008.

Classroom Discipline: Guiding Adolescents to Responsible Independence, Grades 5–9 by Linda Crawford and Christopher Hagedorn. Origins Program, 2009.

The First Six Weeks of School by Paula Denton and Roxann Kriete. Northeast Foundation for Children, Inc., 2000.

How to Talk So Kids Can Learn at Home and in School by Adele Faber and Elaine Mazlish. Simon and Schuster, 1996.

How to Talk So Kids Will Listen & Listen So Kids Will Talk by Adele Faber and Elaine Mazlish. Harper, 1999.

Judicious Discipline by Forrest Gathercoal. Caddo Gap Press, 2004.

The Morning Meeting Book by Roxann Kriete with contributions by Lynn Bechtel. Northeast Foundation for Children, Inc., 2002.

Positive Discipline by Jane Nelsen. Random House, 2006.

The Power of Our Words: Teacher Language That Helps Children Learn by Paula Denton, EdD. Northeast Foundation for Children, Inc., 2007.

Restitution: Restructuring School Discipline by Diane Chelsom Gossen. New View Publications, 1996.

Teaching Children to Care: Classroom Management for Ethical and Academic Growth, K–8 by Ruth Sidney Charney. Northeast Foundation for Children, Inc., 2002.

Working with More Challenging Behaviors

Beyond Time Out: A Practical Guide to Understanding and Serving Students with Behavioral Impairments in the Public Schools, 2nd edition, by John Stewart, PhD. Hastings Clinical Associates, 2002.

The Explosive Child: A New Approach for Understanding and Parenting Easily Frustrated, Chronically Inflexible Children by Ross W. Greene. Harper-Collins, 2001.

Lost at School: Why Our Kids with Behavioral Challenges Are Falling Through the Cracks and How We Can Help Them by Ross W. Greene. Scribner, 2009.

Sammy and His Behavior Problems: Stories and Strategies from a Teacher's Year by Caltha Crowe. Northeast Foundation for Children, Inc., 2010.

The Self-Control Classroom: Understanding and Managing the Disruptive Behavior of All Students, Including Those with ADHD, revised edition, by James Levin and John M. Shanken-Kaye. Kendall/Hunt, 1996.

Setting Limits in the Classroom: How to Move Beyond the Dance of Discipline in Today's Classrooms, revised edition, by Robert J. MacKenzie. Three Rivers Press, 2003.

Solving Thorny Behavior Problems: How Teachers and Students Can Work Together by Caltha Crowe. Northeast Foundation for Children, Inc., 2009.

ACKNOWLEDGMENTS

The ideas and teaching strategies presented in this book have been developed, tested, and refined over the past thirty years by many of our colleagues at Northeast Foundation for Children and by thousands of teachers in a wide variety of classrooms nationwide. The authors wish to express their deepest thanks to all these people for sharing their experiences, for welcoming us into their classrooms and schools, and for always trying to do what's best for children.

At Northeast Foundation for Children, we would like to thank Lynn Bechtel for project management and editing of the second edition, Helen Merena for design of the second edition, and Margaret Berry Wilson for her thoughtful review of the second edition text.

We would also like to thank the Shinnyo-En Foundation for their generous support of the development of this book. The mission of the Shinnyo-En Foundation is "to bring forth deeper compassion among humankind, to promote greater harmony, and to nurture future generations toward building more caring communities."

239

AUTHORS' ACKNOWLEDGMENTS

FROM THE FIRST EDITION

I would like to thank my husband, Peter, for his continual support and sense of humor. I thank my colleagues in the Fitchburg Public Schools for welcoming me into their classrooms and professional lives. In particular, I am grateful to the staff of B. F. Brown Arts Vision Middle School, especially the *Responsive Classroom* Training Team, and the school's principal, Bernie DiPasquale.

—Kathryn Brady

I wish to thank my family, Tim, Tess, and Tyler, for their support and encouragement and their willingness to engage in lively, often humorous conversations about rules.

—Mary Beth Forton

I would like to thank the staff, parents, and children at Heath Elementary. Especially, I would like to thank our teaching assistants Judy Clark, Jill Kuehl, Lynn Kain, Michelle Howe, Deb Lively, Alice Lemelin, Tom Dean, Sandy Gilbert, Robin Jenkins, and Angela Sonntag for their steadfast commitment and love for the children they teach.

—Deborah Porter

 Kathryn Brady has been a teacher for thirty years, specializing in the education of students with emotional impairment. Currently, Kathryn is the principal of Reingold Elementary School in Fitchburg, Massachusetts. Kathryn is a *Responsive Classroom* consulting teacher.

 Mary Beth Forton has taught language arts in elementary and middle schools, specializing in working with students with learning difficulties. She is now director of publications and communications for Northeast Foundation for Children, where she has worked for over twenty years. She is a co-author of *Classroom Spaces That Work*.

 Deborah Porter was a primary grades teacher at Heath Elementary School in Heath, Massachusetts, for many years. She is now a Title One math support teacher in that district. Her thirty-five years in education include teaching at Greenfield Center School and co-founding and teaching at the Heath Preschool. She is a *Responsive Classroom* consulting teacher.

The *Responsive Classroom* approach to teaching emphasizes social, emotional, and academic growth in a strong and safe school community. The goal is to enable optimal student learning. Created by classroom teachers and backed by evidence from independent research, the *Responsive Classroom* approach consists of classroom and schoolwide practices for deliberately helping children build academic and social-emotional competencies.

At the heart of the *Responsive Classroom* approach are ten classroom practices:

Morning Meeting—gathering as a class each morning to greet each other and warm up for the day ahead

Rule Creation—helping students create classroom rules that allow all class members to meet learning goals

Interactive Modeling—teaching children expected behaviors through a unique modeling technique

Positive Teacher Language—using words and tone in ways that promote children's active learning and self-discipline

Logical Consequences—responding to misbehavior in a way that allows children to fix and learn from their mistakes while preserving their dignity

Guided Discovery—introducing classroom materials using a format that encourages independence, creativity, and responsibility

Academic Choice—increasing student motivation and learning by allowing students teacher-structured choices in their work

Classroom Organization—setting up the physical room in ways that encourage students' independence, cooperation, and productivity

Working with Families—involving them as partners and helping them understand the school's teaching approaches

Collaborative Problem-Solving—using conferencing, role-playing, and other strategies to help students resolve problems

Northeast Foundation for Children, Inc., a not-for-profit educational organization, is the developer of the *Responsive Classroom*® approach to teaching. We offer the following for elementary school educators:

Publications and Resources

- Books, CDs, and DVDs for teachers and school leaders
- Professional development kits for school-based study
- Website with extensive library of free articles: www.responsiveclassroom.org
- Free quarterly newsletter for elementary educators
- The *Responsive*® blog, with news, ideas, and advice from and for elementary educators

Professional Development Services

- Introductory one-day workshops for teachers and administrators
- Week-long institutes offered nationwide each summer and on-site at schools
- Follow-up workshops and on-site consulting services to support implementation
- Development of teacher leaders to support schoolwide implementation
- Resources for site-based study
- National conference for administrators and teacher leaders

FOR DETAILS, CONTACT:

Responsive Classroom®

Northeast Foundation for Children, Inc.
85 Avenue A, Suite 204, P.O. Box 718
Turners Falls, Massachusetts 01376-0718

800-360-6332 ■ www.responsiveclassroom.org
info@responsiveclassroom.org

HP1161